TELL IT LIKE IT IS

TELL IT LIKE IT IS

MY STORY

by

AARON NEVILLE

hachette
BOOKS
New York

Hachette Books
Hachette Book Group
1290 Avenue of the Americas
New York, NY 10104
HachetteBooks.com
Twitter.com/HachetteBooks
Instagram.com/HachetteBooks

First Edition: September 2023

Published by Hachette Books, a subsidiary of Hachette Book Group, Inc. The Hachette Books name and logo is a trademark of the Hachette Book Group.

The Hachette Speakers Bureau provides a wide range of authors for speaking events. To find out more, go to hachettespeakersbureau.com or email HachetteSpeakers@hbgusa.com.

Books by Hachette Books may be purchased in bulk for business, educational, or promotional use. For information, please contact your local bookseller or Hachette Book Group Special Markets Department at: special.markets@hbgusa.com.

The publisher is not responsible for websites (or their content) that are not owned by the publisher.

Library of Congress Control Number: 2023936814

ISBNs: 9780306832536 (hardcover); 9780306834141 (B&N signed edition); 9780306832550 (ebook)

Printed in the United States of America

LSC-C

Printing 1, 2023

I've walked through this world sometimes without a friend

My life has been up and down, been close to an end

But I've been through the mill

And I've paid my dues

Walked so many miles in different people's shoes

But I've been through the fire

And I've walked in the rain

I've felt the joy and endured the pain

Once I was a schemer

But I always was a dreamer

But it took me who I was and where I've been

To make me who I am

Contents

TELL IT LIKE IT IS

1

Lord, Get Me Out of Here

I spent some long years running in the wrong direction down a dark path. It took a combination of God, music, and four strong women to truly save my life. The first of those women was my mother, Amelia Landry Neville. She definitely was my first earth angel. She carried me in her womb, I was delivered to her, and she nurtured me and suckled me to her breast. She raised me from birth to seventeen years old. She showed me so much love all my life. I remember how safe I always felt with her.

Mommee taught me all kinds of good things, like manners and respect. She taught me the Golden Rule. She made sure I went to school and to church. She always had a pleasant look on her face. If I had a boo-boo, she made it all better. If I ever had a problem, she was my problem-solver. She always understood me, even when I went astray and didn't understand myself.

My mother turned me on to St. Jude, the patron saint of lost cases. Whenever I was in trouble, she brought me to St. Ann's shrine in Treme, where we would both crawl up the stairs on our knees, saying a prayer on each step until we got to the statue of Jesus at the top. St. Jude has been watching out for me all my life, and I can thank God and Mommee for that.

Another strong, beautiful woman who's been in my life since we were little kids is my sister Athelgra. We've been best friends since we lived in the Calliope Projects. I believe she is one of my guardian angels. She's my younger sister, but she also helped to raise me by always being in my corner, having my back. I could do no wrong in her eyes. Athelgra was my laughing partner, my singing partner. Together, we learned the songs our parents played on the record player, the music Artie, my oldest brother, brought home, and the music we heard on the radio.

When I was sixteen, I met my next earth angel, Joel Roux, who became my wife. She took care of me and watched over me for many, many years. She also kind of raised me. My son Ivan used to say, "Hey, Dad, you know sometimes it's like you're one of the kids." I said I felt the same way. Joel was four foot eleven and a half, but she was a giant. No one messed with her. My trainer in New Orleans, a bodybuilder named Tazzie Colomb who had arms bigger than mine, once said, "I'm scared of that lil woman." Me and Joel had some ups and downs, that's for sure, but we loved each other through it all.

She kept that little boy in me in check. I believe she also gave me a reason for wanting to live.

Sarah Friedman, my present earth angel, came to New Orleans in 2008 to photograph the Neville Brothers, and after the shoot I asked her for her phone number. We started seeing each other, and then we started seeing more of each other. Then we started falling in love. When I met Sarah, I was on a dangerous road. I know she saved my life in all kinds of ways—not just with her love. I'll tell you more about that later on.

The other great constant in my life has been music. Singing was always the thing I loved the best; when I'm singing, that's when I'm happy—more than happy. Whenever I am singing, I am trying to connect with the angels in heaven. I can make the notes so soft and smooth that it would make an angel's wings flutter, and definitely reach God's ears.

One of my favorite things was ending the Neville Brothers shows with "Amazing Grace," which was really a testimony of my life. When I had the audience hypnotized with the swirling notes that God let me be able to do, it was a kind of sacrament. The notes I had in my soul, whenever I was singing each one, would go through my veins like some precious lava. No matter what I was singing, I could feel God in each note coming out of me. My voice was my salvation.

Music, St. Jude, and these four strong women have kept me alive while I wrestled with the other great constant in my life—drugs. I smoked, swallowed, snorted, and injected a large variety of dope for a big part of my life—and I've done a lot of stupid things, crazy things, desperate things to feed that habit.

I started shooting heroin when I was sixteen. It started out just on weekends, with the extra money I made from gigs. I never took it home, and my family didn't know. When Joel and I got married in 1959, she didn't know either, and I made sure it didn't come into my home. Within a year or two, I realized I was on the wrong path, but by then I just couldn't get off it. I'd get too strung out, and then the main thing was to get the bogeys off me.

There were a lot of lonely nights, a lot more adventures—the dangerous kind, playing Russian roulette because you could never be sure what would be in the next bag of dope. A lot of dealers would cut their dope with anything to make it stretch out—powdered milk, sugar, quinine, or worse. It was definitely a risky game. I knew it, but I didn't know how to get off the horse.

In 1972 and '73, when I stayed with my brother Charles in New York City, that had to be one of the worst and most dangerous times in my life. I was thirty-one years old and feeling like I wasn't ever going to have a legit singing career. I'd had a big hit record, *Tell It Like It Is*, in 1966, and spent the next year on the road touring, but a few years later my career had still never jumped the way I'd expected it to.

Back then I could do anything I wanted with my voice. I used to call it connecting the dots, going from one octave to another. I learned some of my singing style from yodeling with the movie cowboys, like Roy Rogers, Gene Autry, Jimmie Rodgers, and the Sons of the Pioneers. But I had no one to listen to me, so I would be frustrated a lot, and I would bring pain to myself by sticking needles in my veins. It was a lonely ride. I was disappointed and angry and just plain tired of waiting for something to happen. Everyone has their own suffering, and me and my junko partners, we sure had ours.

New York City promised what I needed: music, money, and easy dope. Before I moved up to live with Charles, me and my brother Cyril were in a band in New Orleans called Sam and the Soul Machine, with Sam Henry, who was an incredible Hammond B3 organ player. The Soul Machine was the premier band in New Orleans in the late 1960s and early '70s; we played all the local clubs, like the Nite Cap, Desert Sands, the Greystone (which was across the river from New Orleans), and Prout's Club Alhambra, but we never did take off nationally. Plus, I was into the dope pretty good then. Sometimes at the Greystone, the owner paid me with heroin. I never brought it around my house; I'd score with one of my buddies and we'd do up at someone else's house. So I told myself it was okay.

Playing gigs was what I loved, but it just didn't pay enough. To support my family, I had to work on the docks at the Port of New Orleans loading and unloading ships and take on other odd jobs, too. So between the gigging, the working, and the shooting up, it was hard on Joel. She finally had enough and took our four kids and moved back to her parents' house. Losing them nearly killed me right then. Joel's father wouldn't let me see her, or my kids. She said that was the end of us.

In New Orleans, taking care of my family had been the only thing that kept me from sliding all the way into the junkie life. I never shot up around them, and I never brought home the shady guys I was hanging out with. But with my family gone, there was nothing to stop that slide. I knew I was going the wrong way, but I couldn't turn around.

In those days, we didn't even think about rehab. It was something for rich people. And honestly, I was still enjoying the habit. I kicked cold turkey a bunch of times; I'd just curl up in a knot and sweat it out. I'd be clean for a week or two, but then one of my junko partners would come around whistling that infamous little whistle just outside my window, letting me know he had the stuff. I'd hear that whistle and jump up and run to meet him.

Meanwhile, up in New York, Charles was working with bands like Joey Dee and the Starliters and Tony Derringer and the Riverboat Soul Band, which were big acts in those days; plus he was blowing his saxophone with some hardcore jazz guys like George Coleman. Me and Cyril figured there might be better opportunities up there for us. So we went to New York to seek our fortune.

It was a lot easier being a junkie in New York than it was in New Orleans. In New Orleans, the police knew who the guys were in the drug game and targeted them. Back then you could hold a person in jail for seventy-two hours just based on, "You fit the description of a guy," or "You're part of a pending investigation." Seventy-two hours without dope and you were deep in withdrawal, drowning in sweat and twisted in knots. They'd give you a baloney sandwich once in a while, but I didn't have an appetite so I would use it for a pillow.

Every time the shift changed at the police station, they would put you in the paddy wagon and bring you to central lockup, where they paraded you across the lineup stage. If you fit the description of someone they were looking for, you could wind up going to

Louisiana State Penitentiary in Angola. It wasn't just Black men either—they messed with any guy they knew was in the drug game. The great New Orleans musician Mac Rebennack (a.k.a. Dr. John) used to tell us stories about how the police did the same to him.

Charles moved to New York to get away from all that. He had done some time in Angola—for having just two skinny little joints on him. He got out in 1967, after almost four years. He had a couple of petty convictions too—stuff like shoplifting that supported his habit—and the cops put a label on his arrest jacket that said "career criminal." That meant any time he got picked up in New Orleans, his record would show up. Black men were already getting stopped in New Orleans for a little bit of nothing, and Charlie was in the drug game, too. He was once picked out of a lineup for an armed robbery that he didn't do. My daddy got him a lawyer and got him out of it, but it was plenty scary. He knew he had to get out of there. So he escaped to the Big Apple and got a place in Harlem.

When me and Cyril joined him, we lived around 118th Street and Lexington Avenue for a while. New York in the mid-'70s was definitely a different animal. It was some really mean streets. Forty-Second Street and Times Square was full of streetwalkers and head shops and porn theaters. Everybody was doped up and doing something. Harlem was full of empty, falling-down buildings. They were dangerous and scary, but they made good places to shoot up heroin—what we called shooting galleries.

Unlike in New Orleans, the New York police left you alone. They didn't know who we were, anyway—just another couple of Black faces. And it was so easy to get the drugs.

Eventually we moved to a place in Brooklyn on Union Street near Prospect Park. We used to go score in Bedford-Stuyvesant, a neighborhood in Brooklyn that was just crazy with crime in the 1970s and '80s. You'd walk down the steps in an apartment building and have to step over a junkie nodding out. But it was a great place to score dope because it was full of boarded-up buildings that kept you out of sight while you were shooting up; plus we just had no fear back in those days.

I had a running buddy in Brooklyn named Angel. He was a friend of Charles's, and he and I became junko partners. Angel was good at taking stereos out of cars. He used to tell me to play chicky for him—that meant looking out for a bust. Then he'd go up to a car that had one of those little side windows in the front, slip the lock with his jig, open the door, slide in on the floor, and have the stereo out in a minute or two. Angel had been doing this for a long time before I met him, and he was a real expert. He had plenty of connections, too, so he'd have a sale for it right away.

Sometimes we'd find work on the docks in New York, a day here and there. But mostly me and Cyril and Charlie played trio gigs and scored dope and stole things to sell to score more dope—stuff called Blue Magic, Murder One, Body Bag, and all the other dangerous names they'd put on a bag of dope. If you heard someone had OD'd, people asked, "Damn, who he scored from?" because they wanted some. That's how insane it was.

For the trio gigs we took the name the Wild Tchoupitoulas, which was the name of my Uncle Big Chief Jolly's Indian tribe back in New Orleans. The Indian tradition goes way back in the Black communities of New Orleans. The local Indian tribes often took in runaway slaves, and many Black people, including my own family, have some Indian blood in them. The New Orleans Indian groups, called krewes, pay respect to that history with their music and with really fancy costumes they wear called regalia. (The elaborate costumes you see in New Orleans at Mardi Gras are from that tradition.) We wore a less fancy version of the regalia: cut-off jean jackets with rhinestones, beads, and feathers. We looked tough and cool at the same time. We played at clubs uptown, downtown, all over. I remember we were playing at Catch a Rising Star one night, and the MC (he was Richard Belzer, the actor and comedian) said, "When these guys first came in, I thought they were coming to rob us. But after hearing them, I have to say they are great musicians and singers."

God and music were my saving grace—and the dream I kept holding on to that I would be back with my family in New Orleans one day soon. I had this fantasy that maybe if I got famous, if I kicked the dope, if I made a lot of money, I could get them back. That's not where I was headed, though. I knew this was the real rat race, the kind where the rat never gets out of the maze.

In New York we learned how to ride the subway and went all over the city, to all the boroughs. I never robbed anyone there, but I am a big guy and when I got on a subway car, women would pull their pocketbooks in close. I remember one time we scored some dope called Watergate and I nodded out on the subway and missed my stop. I took the train back a few stops, but fell asleep again and ended up doing that a couple of times. I had a box of photos of my family that I carried around, feeling like I was keeping them close, and at some point in all that back and forth, I left it behind. I lost them all. That seemed to be a reflection of what I was doing in my life.

I used to see people walking with their families and felt real bad because I wasn't with mine. I couldn't look at myself in the mirror. When I looked into my eyes, I knew those weren't the same eyes I had as a child. I have a photo of me from back in those days that I'm really ashamed of—a sharp reminder of how low it got. My face is heavy and bloated, but my body is thin and weak. My eyes are half closed, with dark circles under them. I can't stand to see myself like that. I was not the man my mama raised me to be. I was not the big brother who could make my little sister laugh at just about anything. I was not the husband my wife thought she married. I was not the father my kids needed. Someplace deep, I knew I had disappointed all my earth angels. I was praying a lot of hope-to-die prayers because I knew I was in deep trouble. I was praying to St. Jude, because at that time and place I knew I was a hopeless case.

Back then the music was the only thing that kept me sane. Me and Charles and Cyril used to hang out in Prospect Park in Brooklyn or Central Park in Manhattan sometimes and play congas or bongos with the Puerto Rican brothers who were playing out in the park. They really dug Cyril's playing—he sounded like he was straight out of Africa, so they would combine the African and Island beats and end up with something magical. And some days me and Cyril would just walk down the street harmonizing on the songs we heard on the radio. I loved "Me and Julio Down by the Schoolyard" and "Bridge Over Troubled Water" by Simon and Garfunkel, and

Cat Stevens's "Morning Has Broken." Don McLean's song "Starry Night" was out then too. It was about Vincent Van Gogh, and I was identifying with him about not being heard as an artist. Walking down the street singing those songs reminded us that music was what we were supposed to be doing. But it was mostly ripping and running—stealing stuff and getting high.

I remember being down in the boiler room in the basement of one of the brownstones in Harlem where we had been running down the Blue Magic, this great stuff that the Harlem gangsters Frank Lucas and Nicky Barnes brought in from Vietnam. It was all dark and dank there, and it stank from piss, but you didn't care as long as you had a place to do up without the police messing with you. There'd be maybe ten or so other junkies using the boiler room as a shooting gallery, and the stench was unreal. Some would spend their whole day down there; they would do a part of their dope and just hang out so they could nod without prying eyes. Sometimes they used a stocking to tie their arms to get a vein, and the smell of stale blood in that stocking would make a maggot puke—but not a junkie. All they wanted was to see the blood register in the syringe, and that was like heaven. We didn't all have our own works (the needle and syringe), so we'd share, and the guy next to you would say, "Hey, bro, you can use my works, just don't stop them up."

One day I was sitting in that Harlem boiler room waiting for a rig to do my dope with, and I saw this lady lying on the floor. The dope must've been good. Her friend, another lady, was standing over her in a nod, when the one on the floor said in a drawl, "Hey, Mary, I thought I asked you to help me up from here."

Mary said, "Damn, I didn't even know you were down there." It sounded funny at first, but then sad.

I had to see that, I think, so I could learn to have compassion. I'd never really thought about any of the people around me shooting up—what brought them to that place, what might happen to them. I was always just focused on myself, getting what I needed to make the bogeys go away. I can't say they changed me on that day, but that memory stirred something that took hold later, something that helped me open up my heart. Because I saw that, I could understand what they were going through and feel nothing but compassion for them.

I was looking all around that boiler room, so high and so low at the same time, and I knew I was in the bowels of hell, but I just didn't know how to get out. I looked over and saw a wall that had a crack in it that looked like a cross. I started praying to it. I said, "Lord, please get me out of here." But it was a while yet before He rescued me. I still had more running to do. But I know He was carrying me on His shoulders.

One day me and Cyril were doing up with a guy he knew named Diamond. He was just out of the penitentiary, so his system was clean. Diamond shot up first, and he OD'd and went out on the floor. I looked at Cyril and said, "Hey, Chin, you give him mouth-to-mouth while I get my shot." We took turns shooting up and breathing into this guy's mouth until he came around. Now if that wasn't insanity, I don't know what is.

2

The Innocence

When I was born, I came out knees first and almost killed my mother. That was January 24, 1941. And if that wasn't enough, I butted her in her mouth and cracked her tooth while she was holding me in her loving arms. I guess I wasn't easy, even then. But through it all, she still loved me.

Mommee told me that when I was born at the charity hospital in New Orleans, I was a wrinkled-up little red, ugly baby. The doctor asked if she wanted him to remove that big birthmark over my right eye. She said, "Noooo, it's the prettiest thing on him." I'm so glad she did.

We moved to the Calliope (you say it *Callee-ope*) Projects from Valence Street in the Thirteenth Ward when I was one year old, and my earliest memories are there. It was a brand-new project with sturdy brick houses; those St. Joe bricks could withstand anything, so you were safe from hurricanes. One side of the housing project ran along Calliope Street (now Earhart Boulevard), and the whole thing took up about twenty-four city blocks. I'm not exaggerating.

We had a house with two floors—four bedrooms, a living room, a kitchen, and a backyard. It was plenty of room for Mommee and Poppee, Art, Charles, and me. I know much later, in the 1980s, Calliope became really dangerous because of drug gangs. But when we lived there, I always felt safe. It was our paradise, our little world, and I can't imagine growing up anyplace else.

It was like a village; everybody knew everybody. In the Calliope, if you done something stupid you had no business doing, the neighbor had the right to spank you—and you might get another spanking when you got home—but it was because the people there loved you like family. It was all done in love.

There was this big oval park in the center that was our play area. It was maybe the size of two football fields—more than enough space for all us kids to play baseball, football, and anything else we wanted to play. We roller-skated, rode bikes, played marbles, spun tops, made pop guns out of cane reed, made our own kites. There were no electric wires in our park to lose our kites on, and there could be fifty to a hundred kites in the sky some days. Some guys put razors on their kite string to cut other people's strings, but not me.

I was into cowboys back then. After I came home from the movies watching Roy Rogers, Gene Autry, and all the cowboys, I used to yodel like them, and I had a mop stick I named Kemosabe that was my horse. I remember one Mardi Gras Mommee got us a new pair of Roebuck jeans and a plaid shirt and a cowboy hat and used her makeup pencil to draw a mustache on us, and we were cowboys.

We loved to see the Mardi Gras Indians come out in their elaborate costumes and do their Indian dances and chants. It was mesmerizing. Believe it or not, I was also mesmerized watching the garbagemen riding on the back of their truck, jumping off and picking up garbage cans and then emptying them in the back of the truck. I used to say that's what I want to do, but I'm glad I didn't. I guess then I would have been the singing garbageman.

Mommee, Amelia Landry Neville, was beautiful, with high cheekbones and a perpetual smile on her face. She taught us that it was nice to be nice. I still try to look at the world from my mother's eyes. She was street smart, so you couldn't fool her, but she also had the best understanding of what kids felt like and why they did stuff. All my friends used to say, "I wish your mom was my mom."

Poppee, Arthur Neville Sr. (a.k.a. Big Arthur), was big like me. He didn't take no shit. He was left-handed and he'd punch you in the chest with that left hand. One time my friend Marvin was saying some crazy shit and Poppee said, "You think you're a man?"

Marvin said, "Yeah, I'm a man!" and Poppee hit him in the chest.

He crumpled and said, "I'm a little boy."

Poppee could be tough, but we felt protected when we were with him.

I think I heard my father raise his voice to my mother only one time. Just hearing it did something to me, though, because now I can't stand any kind of conflict. It messes with my equilibrium.

Something else happened too, when I was about eight or nine years old. I was on my way to the Gem Theater to see a movie, and I saw this man beating up this woman. She was a hefty barroom lady, but she couldn't stand up to him. He was hitting her in the face and she was bleeding. I wanted to run over there and hit him, but he would've beat my ass. I didn't enjoy the movie that day, and I swore I would never hit a woman. I've kept to that one.

I couldn't have had a better childhood. If we were poor, we didn't know anything about it. Mommee saw to that. I thought I was rich if I had a pocket full of marbles. Sometimes we had to put cardboard in our shoes because the ball bearings in our roller skates made holes in them, but all the kids in the projects had cardboard in their shoes or patches on their knees from playing marbles or spinning tops in the dirt. Now they're paying big bucks for holey pants, but Mommee used to patch the holes in ours.

We always had food to eat, even if it was stretching a pot of red beans or collard greens. Sometimes you'd see the ladies out on the medians between the houses (we called it neutral ground) stooped over to pick something called pepper grass, which they would add to the greens to make more.

The vegetable man used to come through the projects on a horse-drawn buggy selling fruits and vegetables he got from the French Market. He wore his cap acey-deucey to the side—we called that raddy—and he had a sidekick to holler out about his wares. "I got watermelon, lady, red to the rind, oh lady, come see how nice, got the red watermelon and it's cold on ice. I got cabbage, lady, I got the good sweet corn, I got sweet potatoes, I got Irish potatoes. I got apples, lady, I got peaches and pears." The ladies would come out to see what kind of bargain they could get, and he would cut a plug out of the watermelon to let them get a taste. The vegetable man always gave the ladies a little something. We called that "lagniappe"—a Creole word that means "a little extra."

The housing authority would come to our park area to cut the grass, and they would leave big piles of grass clippings. I just loved diving into them. I had asthma as a kid, but I never realized that the cut grass would be a trigger for it. Quite a few times my family was getting ready to go somewhere, and my asthma would either have me all swollen or just having trouble breathing, so I had to stay home.

My mother's mother, Maw Maw, had asthma too, and she knew just what to do. One time she saw that my asthma was blocking my breathing and she put her mouth over my nose and cleared it with her mouth. Now that's a thing called love.

Maw Maw couldn't speak clear English, but you knew what she was saying in her Creole/broken English. Maw Maw, my mother, her brother George (Big Chief Jolly) Landry, and my aunties all spoke Creole when they didn't want us to know what they were talking about, but they didn't teach it to us because they wanted us to speak good English. We only learned the cuss words. Our great-great-grandmother came from the island of Martinique and moved to a place called Convent, Louisiana. None of them spoke much English. They spoke French or broken French—patois, they called it—with a mixture of Native American Choctaw.

When I was growing up, Poppee and Uncle Jolly went to sea on a merchant marines ship. It was during World War II, and it was plenty dangerous—they got torpedoed one time, and their ship was almost sunk. I guess Mommee understood that, but we kids didn't, so we missed Poppee and Uncle Jolly but we weren't really worried about them. About the only thing I remember from the war was we used to have blackouts where all the lights went out, and then these big searchlights would shine across the sky looking for enemy airplanes.

When they were gone, Mommee took care of us, along with our grandmothers. Mommee was the greatest, kindest woman, and she made all us kids feel like royalty. She read us stories, played games with us, helped us do jigsaw puzzles, sang to us. She took care of our boo-boos and made them all better.

Sometimes we played a game called smut. It was a card game where the loser got a big puff of flour on their face. Sometimes we would take blankets and drape them over the sofa and make a cave, and sometimes we would slide down the stairs on a piece of cardboard or a blanket.

My dad and Uncle Jolly would bring home all kinds of stuff for us, like every kind of chewing gum Wrigley's made. They would give us beautiful conch shells that we could hear the ocean in.

Artie, three years older than me, had a rep for being a great singer—and for kicking ass. I remember at St. Monica's Catholic School one time this big, tall dude fucked with Artie in the school-yard. Artie jumped up and punched him in the mouth and knocked his teeth through his tongue. Then he put the guy on the handlebars of his bike and took him to the charity hospital. That was the way he was.

Artie grew up to be a great keyboard player, a great singer, a great big brother, and, oh yeah, a great fighter. Once the leader of a local gang and his boys tried to corner Artie. These older dudes, who were dope fiends, saw what was happening and stepped in. They said, "No, it ain't going down like this. He'll fight y'all one at a time." And Artie took turns kicking their asses one by one.

He didn't start fights, but he would win them. His reputation was great protection for me. I would walk around the schoolyard and mess with guys and say, "You fuck with me, I'll get Artie for your ass."

My brother Charlie was next. He was two years older than me. Then my sister Athelgra came in 1944, when I was three. My parents used to block the staircase so she wouldn't fall, and I taught her how to get around the barricades. I used to tie a little towel around the neck of Athelgra's dolls and make them fly like Superman and Batman. We rode the bus together to Bush Elementary School, and this little boy who had a crush on her used to pay me a nickel to let him sit by her. It was the only pimping I ever did.

Me and Athelgra were, and still are, close as two peas in a pod. We would laugh at the drop of a hat, at nothing. Mommee would come in and tell us to stop all that laughing, but we couldn't. Mommee would say, "Stop or I'll get a belt," and before you knew it she was on the floor laughing with us.

It kept up all the way to when our father, who we loved dearly, died in 1967. At his funeral we were in the front row at the church, and one of the deacons got up and started to stutter, and God forgive us, Athelgra started laughing. As soon as I saw her, I started too. The ladies of the church thought she was fainting with grief and started to fan her and give her smelling salts, and she just laughed harder.

On the subject of church, we used to go to a segregated church where the Blacks had to sit in the back. One Sunday there was no room in the back pews, so me and Athelgra sat in a pew around the middle of the church. All the heads popped around, staring at us, and even the priest stopped preaching to stare at us. So I grabbed Athelgra's hand and left, and it was a while before I went back. That's the way it was in those days—and it seems like some would like to have it that way again. I never stopped praying, though. And now I live with the Holy Spirit in my heart and soul. I always say, "Stay straight with the house."

I was seven when my brother Cyril was born. I was still turning Athelgra's baby dolls into Superman then. I used to call her doll a sloppyback alligator with a swingy tail. Who knows where kids get that stuff from?

Charles used to babysit us; he would tie us up and put a gag in our mouths and put us in the closet and tell us we were playing cowboys. Then he'd lie on the couch and read. My mother would come home from work and say, "Where's the kids, Charles?" And he'd say, "Oh, they're upstairs in the closet."

He used to play Tarzan with me, and one time he jumped down off the banister with a knife and cut me in my chest. It was an accident, but I had a scar for a long time. When one of my baby teeth got loose, he'd tie a string to it and the other end to the doorknob and slam the door, and the tooth would pop out.

Charles used to experiment with things and invent stuff and make these cool model airplanes. He had the highest IQ in our school and wanted to be a scientist, but one of the nuns told him he shouldn't think like that; that he should be an auto mechanic or a brick mason instead. It really got in his head, and he was crushed. It turned him back to his horn, though, which turned out not to be a bad thing.

Despite what they said to Charles, I have good memories of St. Monica's Catholic School. It was always a safe place for me. The nuns were like my parents away from home. Between them and my mother, I was taught morals—something the world is lacking today a lot. Like every school in New Orleans at the time, St. Monica's was segregated. But at the public schools Black teachers taught Black kids. At St. Monica's, the white sisters taught Black students. And they took some serious judgment for it. There were times they had to run from the Klan or got death threats. That taught me a lot about not judging people.

We paid about a dollar a year to go to St. Monica's, and that was where I got my first job—cleaning the boys' and the girls' bathrooms. I was proud of my job, and I made enough to keep me in candy and marbles. Me and my brothers also used to go to the housing authority and get those push lawn mowers and make money cutting people's grass. We made a wagon out of wooden apple crates and old wagon wheels to bring people's groceries home from the HG Hill grocery store and made some change that way too.

I was eleven when my little sister Cookie was born in 1952. Her real name was Rowena, named after Poppee's mother. Cookie was

never really healthy. She had an enlarged heart and needed an oper-
ation on her thyroid. She ended up with keloid scars that looked like
a necklace around her neck. Despite all that, she was always smiling. She used to say to me and my brothers, "Oh, you're so handsome, I want to marry you." Cookie had a hard time, but she didn't
sit around complaining about it.

That same year, when I was in sixth grade, I stood in front of my
class and recited a poem that I had to learn called "Lovely Lady
Dressed in Blue, Teach Me How to Pray." Later on in my life when
I really needed prayer, I put music to it and recorded it on my album
To Make Me Who I Am. By then it was like someone was telling me
how to sing it, like that little boy in me was begging the Blessed
Mother to teach me how to pray. But that was a long time later.

When I was about twelve, me and my friends started venturing
out of the projects. One time me and Sonny, who lived next door
from us, went to see the great singer, piano player, and band leader
Tommy Ridgley. He was playing on a flatbed truck on Claiborne
Avenue. At the time, he had a song out called "Ooh Lawdy My
Baby" that had a sort of a rhumba beat to it. I was a big fan. New
Orleans was full of music, and it was easy to find.

About the worst thing that happened to me in those years was
related to my first bad habit—smoking. I started smoking L&Ms
when I was about twelve. Me and my boys thought we were so cool.
I used to carry these strike-anywhere matches in my back pocket to
light my cigarettes. One day I was sitting on the concrete porch with
Jenny, this girl I was liking at the time, and her sister Katherine. We
were just shooting the breeze when all of a sudden, I got an itch on

my butt and scratched it and ignited those matches. My pants caught on fire and I had to take them off in front of Jenny and her sister. They laughed at me for a whole year. But I laughed too—it was pretty funny.

One day I was walking with my buddies and smoking a cigarette, and my mother appeared from nowhere. My friends turned around to say hello to her, and when they turned back, that cigarette was gone. If I was to see any of my boys today, they would ask me, "Damn, Aaron, what happened to that cigarette?" And I'd tell them, "I swallowed it."

3

Neville Family Music

If you're born in New Orleans, there's music when you come into the world, music when you go out, and music all the time in between. My brother Artie once told me that when I was a baby in the crib, I would stand up and go "Aaaaaaaah" till I fell asleep. I guess I was trying to sing even then.

As for the going out, I remember I'd be in the park in the Calliope playing marbles or tops and we'd hear the drums of the second liners—the bands following funerals—and run toward the music. (The first line following the coffin is the family of mourners, and the second line is the musicians and the people following the music.) They'd play that slow dirge on the way to the graveyard, and then something cranked up on the way back to send them off right. We all knew the music, and we'd follow the second line and dance.

That's the only way to send someone off—mourn them, yes, but also celebrate their life.

Before we were born, Mommee and Uncle Jolly were the best song-and-dance team in New Orleans. They had a chance to go on the road with Louis Prima, but Maw Maw wouldn't let them go because of the Jim Crow laws. She said they wouldn't have been treated right, and it could be downright dangerous. Because of that, Mommee said she would never stop any of us from following our dreams—and she never did.

I remember sitting on the floor in our house in the Calliope watching Mommee and Uncle Jolly doing the lindy hop, with Uncle Jolly throwing Mommee between his legs and over his back. The music was probably something by Louis Jordan. When he and Mommee danced it looked like a lot of fun, so Mommee taught all us kids how to dance. Later, when I started going to parties, the guys used to stand around while the girls danced with each other. But I knew how to dance, so it was a whole different game for me.

Uncle Jolly had pretty teeth and an infectious smile. He had a ratty walk, kind of hipty dipty, that was real cool, and I used to try to imitate it.

My mother sang all the time around the house. She was a big fan of Sarah Vaughan and Dinah Washington. My dad sang in a baritone in the bathtub—he loved this song called "Orange Colored Sky" that Nat King Cole recorded. But his real talent was that he could whistle like all the different birds. None of us could do it like he did. I wish now I could whistle like him, but it's impossible.

I remember sitting on Maw Maw's lap when I was five or six while she listened to the gospel station on the radio: Dr. Daddyo was the DJ, and we'd listen to Mahalia Jackson, Brother Joe May, the Blind Boys. I liked to sing along, but it was some hard singing; it sounded to me almost like screaming. My mom and dad were big Nat King Cole fans, and I liked that better. Poppee had every record Nat King Cole made. He worked on the trains as a pullman porter for a time, so he loved the song "Route 66" because he kind of knew that route. I loved it when Nat King Cole sang "Mona Lisa." He was so smooth, and his diction was so great. I used to pretend I was him, walking around singing and holding my comb like it was a microphone.

I used to sing my way into the movies too. I'd go to the Gem Theater to see all the cowboy and Tarzan movies, and they'd say, "Sing for us, little Aaron." I'd sing "Wheel of Fortune" or "Mona Lisa," and they'd let me in for free. After I came home from the cowboy movies, I would come back to the projects and yodel all over the park. People heard that yodeling and they knew it was me. I used to call it vocal gymnastics.

My oldest brother, Artie, worked at Tickle's Record Shop. He would bring home records by Sonny Til and the Orioles, the Clovers, the Swallows, Billy Ward and His Dominoes, Hank Ballard and the Midnighters. They had songs that they wouldn't play on the radio because they weren't G-rated, like "Work with Me Annie," "Annie Had a Baby," and "I Love Your Sexy Ways."

Guys used to hang out around the Calliope and sing. There was a group called the Del-Royals that included Calvin LeBlanc and

Willie Harper, who became pretty famous. Years later, in 1960, I shared a split recording session with them for Minit Records.

Artie had a doo-wop group that sang harmonies out on the park benches at night. They were around fifteen or sixteen then, and they called themselves the Notes. They would win all the talent shows and get all the prize money and the girls. Those harmonies sounded to me like the sweetest things on earth, so I wanted to sing with them, but they used to run me away because I was too little. But then one evening one of the guys—his name was Isacher Gordon and we called him Izzy Koo—he said to me, "Hey, Kevin, come here and sing this note." I don't know why he called me Kevin, but he could call me anything as long as they let me sing with them. I could hold those high notes, pure and sweet, and they finally let me in the group. I was maybe ten or eleven and I was thrilled. Artie and Izzy Koo showed me how to do all of the harmonies, and I was on a cloud. The first song I sang with them (I still remember it) was "Sunday Kind of Love" by the Harptones. It was on then. I was singing with the big boys—no turning back.

I couldn't think of nothing else but singing. I was cool singing just to myself, thinking, "Wow, I can sing just like some of my heroes." My voice would soothe me, so I started wanting to soothe other people with it as well. I can't say why, but the high singing always touched me, and I wanted to touch people myself with those high notes.

I started singing for the company when my parents had people over. Anyone who wanted to hear me sing was good enough for me. The Notes would sit out on a bench in the Calliope and sing just about every evening. Half the projects would gather around us, listening. At the time I was liking this girl named Jeanie who lived next door. She had the most beautiful dark chocolate skin, smooth as silk, and I would show off for her, hitting the high notes. We called each other boyfriend and girlfriend (I didn't even know what sex was at that age) and it was just a great feeling knowing that she liked me.

When I was in school, my mind and my heart were preoccupied with the music I was hearing. I always had a song going through my head. I remember when I rode the bus to school, the driver always had the radio on. I heard "Rhapsody in Blue," I heard "The Wheel of Fortune"—all kinds of things. Back then I could learn a song after hearing it just a few times; it would get stuck in my head. Sometimes I'd get kept after school for singing and beating on my desk.

My sister Athelgra was my singing partner at home. We sang all the time—while washing and drying the dishes or hanging up the clothes outside on the line. One time, after we moved uptown, we were doing our chores and harmonizing, and our aunt who lived next door knocked on the wall and said, "Y'all turn that radio down!"

Athelgra used to sing with a bunch of her friends in high school: Barbara Ann and Rosa Lee Hawkins, who were sisters, plus their cousin Joan Marie Johnson. They eventually formed a group called the Dixie Cups. She didn't decide to start her professional singing career until much later and now, when she's all grown up (and then some), she's a member of the Dixie Cups. They sang backup on my album *Bring It on Home*.

I remember when Charlie got his first saxophone. Auntie Cat, my dad's mother's sister, bought it for him when he was eleven—a real pretty one named Selmer (that was the maker). The first time he started blowing, there were no honks or squeaks, just clear notes. He was a natural. When the nuns at St. Monica's Catholic School told him he couldn't be a scientist, that really put his head somewhere else and turned him back to his horn. Four years later, when he was just fifteen, he left home to play with the Rabbit's Foot Minstrel Show. Mommee had to sign a paper to let him go. He was billed as the boy wonder on the sax, and he played blues clubs with people like B.B. King, Jimmy Reed, and Bobby Blue Bland. He got a head start learning his horn with these hard hitters. Later on, Charles joined the navy and was stationed in Memphis, so he got to play on Beale Street with all the blues guys.

Cyril ended up being an amazing singer, percussionist, and funkster extraordinaire. Since he was seven years younger than me, me and Cyril really started our jam after we moved out of the projects. All this time Cyril would sit by the door and watch and listen when Artie and his band rehearsed, absorbing it all. He got started drumming by beating on hubcaps and park benches with a stick. When he did jump out, he was like dynamite. In junior high school he started to sing and play the drums in talent shows. He and our friend Howard Guidry (a.k.a. Pitty Pat) used to go up against each other. (Me and Pitty Pat still talk all the time.) Pitty Pat would do Jackie Wilson and Cyril would do James Brown as good or better than the original. He could do the dance, the split—everything.

A lot of people in the Calliope played instruments, and they would sit outside and make great music. Red Tyler, the great sax player, lived next door to us, and he and Charles used to hang out and play together. Red was already married and had a daughter named Jernelle. I was in love with his wife, Leona. One day his wife went to visit his mother, and she just dropped dead on the front porch. His mother came out and died as well. It was a deep time— he lost his wife and his mother on the same day. I was about eleven then, and I didn't know what to think. I saw everybody had tears, and I was sad too, but I'm not sure I really understood what had happened.

It was like that again when Maw Maw died when I was thirteen. She lived with us then, and me and my sister found her dead in her bed with her rosary in her hand and a smile on her face. That was the closest to us that death had come.

When we moved uptown, the great drummer Clarence Brown (a.k.a. Junie Boy) lived next door, and Cyril used to play with him. When Clarence grew up, he became the drummer for Fats Domino. We all went to school with Leo Morris, who later became a famous drummer and changed his name to Idris Muhammad, and Cyril used to play with him too.

At St. Monica's we had a drum-and-bugle corps, and I played both. The pastor showed me how to play the instruments, and I just picked them up. Me and Art started playing the piano, too, just by jumping on whenever we were at somebody's house who had one. Auntie Lealah had a piano, so we could go there and play. They had an organ at Trinity Church over in the Thirteenth Ward where my great-aunts went, and that's where Artie fell in love with the sound of the Hammond B3. I remember the first time he touched the organ, it made such a big sound that it scared him. But it was on then, and he just took to it after that.

Uncle Jolly was also a piano player and showed us a couple of things. Art showed me a couple of things too, but I never did take any piano lessons or learn how to read music. I can read chord changes, but I played by ear then and I still do. It's a style my Uncle Jolly called funky knuckle. Mostly, we all just figured it out on our own.

Nobody in the family could read music except Charles. We learned by listening and watching and playing. Music was in our blood. It was in our hearts. It was in our souls. It was in our family.

4

Mole Face and Melvin

This is the saga of Aaron (a.k.a. Mole Face) and Melvin. When I was about six years old, Great-Auntie Cat (we called her that because she fed all the stray cats in the neighborhood; she called them God's voiceless children) and her sisters, Aunty Espy and Aunty Lealah, went to Trinity Methodist Church. The church used to take everyone out to picnics at Abita Springs in Waveland, Mississippi, where they had a swimming pool Black people were allowed to use. (Oh yes, the swimming pools were segregated.) We had to take the streetcar uptown to the Thirteenth Ward, where the church was, and then Mr. Kennedy drove the church bus out to Abita Springs.

Melvin Wright lived across the corner from the church. He was about the same age as me. He and I would sit next to each other on the bus, our feet dangling down 'cause we couldn't reach the floor. We didn't utter a word, but every time I went up there to go on a picnic, we would sit together, and we bonded silently, like blood brothers.

Auntie Cat had a house Uptown and another one next door to her on Valence Street that we moved into in 1954. I was thirteen and had just graduated from eighth grade. It was a two-story double shotgun house. Shotgun houses are narrow and deep, and a double is twice as wide. They called them shotgun houses because you could stand at the front door and shoot a shotgun and it would go straight through to the back door.

That's when me and Melvin really hooked up and started our journey as Mole Face and Melvin. You seen one, you seen the other. We were both quiet and didn't need to say much, but we had each other's back from day one. Pretty soon we started venturing out of our neighborhood, and before you knew it we were doing shit we shouldn't have. I guess you could say that was the end of my innocence.

We went to parties all over New Orleans, and that included going into other hoods looking for girls. The girls all dug me and Melvin, but a lot of times the guys in those hoods didn't like the idea of us coming through there talking to their girls, so they'd challenge us. Well, we liked going searching for girls. And anyway, Melvin took no shit from anybody. Plus we liked to fight. It was an adrenaline rush. Melvin always had a little grin on his face when we were fighting. So we would get into fights with those dudes. And we'd kick ass. The guys we fought gave us the nickname Mole Face and Melvin. They thought I was offended by being called Mole Face, but I loved it.

We didn't look for trouble, but it would find us and we didn't run from it. We ran toward it, defying it. We walked through different neighborhoods, building our reps and welcoming any fight. And we earned respect everywhere.

A few months later Marvin Metoyer moved into our neighborhood. He was a year older than us and lived with his grandmother and his uncle. We all just clicked, and from jump street, we were like brothers. We were all the same size and height—three tall, skinny kids—so I guess we looked a little like brothers. The three of us didn't have to join no gang because we were the gang.

Despite my many extracurriculars with Melvin and Marvin, music was still what I loved best. I would have an eargasm listening to music. I loved all kinds. I first heard Sam Cooke when I was thirteen years old; he sang a hymn called "Any Day Now" (I later recorded it on one of my gospel albums), and I dug his style to the utmost. He became like a god to me; I followed his every note.

When we moved uptown, I was turned on to groups like the Heartbeats (their big hit was "A Thousand Miles Away"), who later called themselves Shep and the Limelites. There were groups like the Turbans, with hits like "When You Dance," "Let Me Show You," and "Congratulations." Then there was Little Anthony and the Imperials, with "Tears on My Pillow," the Moonglows (Marvin Gaye's first group; years later I read Marvin Gaye's book, and it turned out he and I were listening to the same singers), the Five Satins, and the Platters. Artie and Izzy Koo turned me on to the Harptones ("A Sunday Kind of Love") and Sonny Til and the Orioles ("It's Too Soon to Know"). Now that I think of it, a lot of the groups had bird names, like the Crows and the Flamingos. Artie and Izzy Koo said that's because they sang bird harmonies. The Flamingos were one of my all-time favorites. They had that smooth harmony with the reverb on the vocals, with songs like "I Only Have Eyes for You."

I remember the first time I heard Clyde McPhatter, I was mesmerized. He had that high tenor voice that was like medicine to my soul. He sang with Billy Ward and His Dominoes, and later with the Drifters, until he went solo. I was also a big fan of Pookie Hudson and the Spaniels ("Goodnite Sweetheart"), and years later I got to meet him. He told me how they got their name. Before they were famous, they were rehearsing in the garage and one of the wives hollered down, "You sound like a pack of dogs!" That's why they're named after a dog instead of a bird.

I guess you could say doo-wop—those sweet, smooth, smoky harmonies—was my first love. So in 1955, when I was at Samuel J. Green Junior High School, I started a doo-wop group with a couple of other students—Reynelle Hall, Wallace George, William McQuartz, Ursula Gray, and Evelyn Dent. We would sing live on the radio sometimes, stuff like "Stormy Weather," "Earth Angel," and "In the Still of the Night," which was the biggest doo-wop record of all time.

There was a certain hairstyle associated with doo-wop that we called konk, where guys would straighten their hair and then put waves in it. All the big groups had konks, and I couldn't wait to get mine.

Konk was what we called the chemical hair relaxer congolene, which was mostly lye, a really corrosive chemical. In the homemade version, you'd mix it with something like eggs and potatoes to make a paste that would stay in your hair. You'd leave it on for a little while, then rinse it out real good. I remember when we were still living in the Calliope, Uncle Jolly had a jar of konk grease in our medicine cabinet, so I used to put a little bit in my hair before going to school. The kids at school just thought I had semigood hair.

The konk grease could sometimes turn your hair a little red. It could also burn a hole in your head, so you paid for your wave. In his movie about Malcolm X, Spike Lee put in a scene where Malcolm was getting a konk and the police shut off the water; it started to burn and he stuck his head in the toilet. That happened to my Uncle Jolly when he was in the merchant marines (my dad would never konk his head). He was on the ship when the water went off.

For my first real konk, I had a style called the Ivanhoe, with the hair combed to the front. Later I had the Quo Vadis, which was similar but with your hair combed to the side. Tim, the head barber who did the konks at the local salon, did it for me. I used to hang out and watch how he did it and then go uptown and practice on Marvin's and Melvin's heads. Now that we're all grown up, Marvin sometimes tells me he's gonna call a lawyer because I am the reason he has no hair now. I don't think that's true, but you never know, because I used to konk his hair when I was high, so he got what he got.

Back in the day, they called straight hair good hair, so dudes would get fried, dyed, and laid to the side no matter what it did to their head. But when Black folks started wearing our hair more natural in the 1960s, there was this joke going around that if someone with good hair stood next to someone with an Afro and bricks fell on their heads, it probably would bounce off the Afro and the good hair wouldn't protect them.

When I was fifteen I was still going to parties, dances, sock hops, roller-skating, still being a child, still making new friends. But I also got my first real gig. It was at a place in the French Quarter on Bourbon and Toulouse Streets called the Driftwood Lounge. Art Jones, an upright bass player, had an all-blind band that included Snooks Eaglin on guitar and vocals, Boy Blue on sax, and me on piano and vocals. Snooks sometimes played with my brother Artie's band, the Hawketts, and he got me the gig. We played a lot of covers, from Fats Domino to Elvis, and all the doo-wop songs. It was a great first gig. Because I was only fifteen, Mommee had to sign a paper giving me permission to work there.

Since I was the only one in the band who could see, it was my job to go out on Bourbon Street and get them their foot-long hot dogs. That's because, like all clubs in the French Quarter, the Driftwood Lounge was white-only and we couldn't eat there. Black musicians might play at a white club (not that uncommon in New Orleans), but we had to come in through the back door and leave as soon as we were done. During intermission, we had to stay on the stage.

They didn't allow mixed bands with Black and white musicians either. And white patrons were not allowed in Black clubs. This wasn't just the custom; it was the law. And it was enforced. Later on when Art and Charles played at the Dew Drop Inn, a Black club, Dr. John (who was white) would sometimes sit in with the band or come to see a musician he wanted to hear. More than once the police hauled him off to jail. I remember one time as they were leading him out he told them, "Y'all will have to come back again next week and get me, because Ray Charles is going to be here and I'm definitely coming to see him."

Some restaurants and shops had outside windows where Black people could buy stuff, but we were not allowed inside. At some grocery stores they'd throw your change at you because they didn't want to touch your hand. My schools were all segregated, and the teachers were all Black, except at St. Monica's.

Segregation in New Orleans, in Louisiana, in the South, was a fact of life, and not one we really paid much attention to. It was just the way you lived. There was an invisible line you did not cross, places you didn't go, neighborhoods you didn't walk through, stores you didn't enter, because you knew you weren't welcome. Emmett Till and I were both fourteen years old when he was lynched, and at the time Mommee was scared for me. I remember people were saying, "That's what happens when a guy goes someplace he's not supposed to go."

There were some white people who had businesses in our neighborhood who were really nice and respected everybody. And musicians are usually all about the music and don't care about that other shit. But it was an individual thing. Officially, legally, New Orleans was strictly segregated.

The clubs didn't really start to be integrated until the 1970s, when the Neville Brothers started playing at Tipitina's. Before that, Tipitina's had an outside window where Black folks could be served food, but we couldn't go inside. I don't think it fully changed until Jazz Fest started in 1976 and everyone came to play together on the stages and be together in the audience.

Anyway, I played with that blind band for about a month, and it was exciting for me to be up there doing what I loved to do and hear people clapping for me.

Back in 1954 Artie and the Hawketts recorded "Mardi Gras Mambo," and it's still played every Mardi Gras as a kind of New Orleans anthem. The band was Artie on vocals and piano, my brother Charlie, George Davis, and Morris Bechamin on sax, Roy Evans on bass, Alfred August on guitar, Israel Bell (a.k.a. Sticks) and J. C. Goods on trumpet, and John Boudreaux on drums. In 1956, when I was sixteen, they let me sing with them. I was in heaven being on the stage with these guys.

We played at school dances, fraternities, and places like that, plus we had a semiregular gig at a place called the Autocrat Club, and another one at the Pimlico Club on Broad Street, where Tommy Ridgley, the bandleader I really liked, also played. They had a waitress there named Irma Thomas who could really sing, and sometimes Tommy or Artie would call her up onstage to sing with them. Her boss eventually fired her for not spending all her time waitressing, but Allen Toussaint heard about her and recorded her, and she's still known as the Soul Queen of New Orleans.

The Hawketts were the premier band in New Orleans, but not the only band. Allen Toussaint, Snooks Eaglin, and the clarinet player Frank Morgan had a seven-piece band called the Flamingos that was our competition.

When I graduated to Walter L. Cohen Senior High School in 1957, Leo Morris, who went to the same school, helped get me another gig. The high school music teacher, Solomon Spencer, put together a couple of bands made up of students, all of them called the Avalons. We'd do covers of Fats Domino, Elvis Presley, Little Richard, the Avalons. We played fraternity parties and high school dances and things like that. Leo was the drummer, and he recommended me. That teacher was making good money off those bands, but he was the only one who was. We made about twenty dollars a gig. Enough to score dope with.

For my sixteenth birthday, I gave myself a present that has lasted all my life. I got the tattoo on my face. My school buddy Jason Pickett came around, we sat down on my parents' back steps, he tied two needles to a matchstick, and he put the tattoo on my cheek. It's a dagger. Some people see it as a cross, and it was one thought away from being a skull and crossbones. Don't ask me why I did it. I don't even know the answer. I guess stupid was set in place at that age.

When my father came home, he was pissed to the highest of pisstivity. He made me scrub it with a Brillo pad and Octagon soap. The skin came off, but the tattoo stayed.

That was around about the same time me and Melvin started stealing cars. They were so easy to steal back then. All you needed was the silver paper from a cigarette pack, put it on the three screws behind the ignition and put it in neutral, and the car started.

We were just joyriding in people's cars, or going to dances or football games or picking up girls. We would always bring the cars back close to where we took them from—if we didn't get busted or into a wreck. We rolled (got away with it) a lot more than we got busted, so we didn't walk too many places.

Around 1957 Marvin's brother, Johnny, moved to New Orleans and joined us in that and many other extracurricular activities. I remember one time me and Marvin and Johnny had stolen a car and me and Johnny wanted to go one place and Marvin wanted to go someplace else. So Marvin started yelling, "Help, this is a stolen car! I know it's stolen because I stole it." Me and Johnny ran, and Marvin took off in the car.

Melvin and Marvin and me boosted cars until I was nineteen. We would be walking down the street singing "Ruby Baby" by the Drifters or "I'm So Glad" by Sam Cooke and the Soul Stirrers while looking for a car to boost.

In 1957, Melvin moved down to the Ninth Ward, where his dad, Big Melvin, built a house. But we still hung out together all the time. One time Melvin and another guy from the Ninth Ward burglarized a money order man's car and got about $20,000. I remember he came to my house and threw all that cash on the bed. Me and Athelgra were home, and we just went WOW! None of us had ever seen that much money. Melvin used some of it to buy me a car, a used 1954 Ford, from a guy he knew who was selling it. That was my first car, but I didn't have it for long. It broke down pretty quick and I didn't know how to fix it. So it was back to boosting rides.

Artie was the straight arrow, and he used to get really mad about us doing stupid stuff like that. Mommee used to just sit me down and tell me about the Golden Rule and what I should be doing. But I had a one-track mind and wanted to do what I wanted to do and didn't mind if it got me in trouble.

I remember one time when we were about sixteen or seventeen, we stole a couple of cars and drove to a football game up in Hahnville, Louisiana, between Xavier Prep (Joel's school) and a school out there. There were thirteen of us from the Thirteenth Ward, and after the game we went to a local dance club. Marvin was dancing with a girl, and this dude came out with all of his boys, grabbed the girl, and said, "Fuck this chump."

We all said, "Marvin, swing on him," and Marvin gave him a punch. And then we all started fighting. Us Thirteenth Ward boys were pretty tough, and those guys were trying to run out the front door. But we had a guy with us named Big Henry (a.k.a. the Ice Man, because he brought his ice hooks with him wherever he went), and he stood at the door and wouldn't let nobody out.

We fought in that place until everyone was down except us. Then we walked outside where the girls were, and they all said I was the boss.

The thing is, we went back there a couple of times later on and got to be friends with all those guys. Back in the day, a fight was just what it was—a fight. You had a fight and then it was over. Not like today where if a guy gets into a fight, somebody comes back and kills the other guy.

One time when I was sixteen me and Melvin were down in the Ninth Ward, where he lived. It was a tough area, so I had his Uncle

Willard's .38 snub nose revolver in my pocket. I never carried a gun, so I'm not sure why I had it that night. We had been taking goofballs (Nebutal, a barbiturate), Red Devils (secobarbital, another barbiturate), and Christmas Trees (Tuinal, a barbiturate that came in a capsule with little red and green balls inside), so I was feeling really goofy. We were in this sweet shop, and I was standing by the jukebox with my hands in my pockets. I couldn't hardly see the records, I was so high. I felt these hands on my shoulder, and I thought it was Melvin wanting to introduce me to someone, when this big, tall dude turned me around and punched me in my mouth and cracked two of my teeth. I ran my tongue over the spot and freaked out. My teeth were cracked! That's all I could think about.

I saw Melvin running toward the dude and it was like everything was going in slow motion. I yelled, "Stay back, Melvin!" and automatically my hand came out of my jacket pocket with the gun and I just shot the guy twice. He looked at me as if he was saying, "Hey bro, why you shot me?" Me and Melvin walked out the sweet shop like Cagney and Bogart, all cool, and then we ran all the way to the Desire Projects and hung out in someone's hallway until the next morning. We didn't know if the guy was dead or not, and we kept listening for some news of a guy being killed.

Mommee used to say, "Don't do anything you're going to regret later," and I finally had an idea of what she meant. I was so scared that night. I was really hoping I didn't kill him. (I wouldn't find out until much later.) I never carried a gun after that.

I didn't go looking for trouble, but I didn't run from it either. And it's not like I enjoyed beating people. When I was fighting someone, I'd be feeling sorry for them, too. Sometimes people got hurt bad in fights, sometimes killed. I remember one night these guys were looking to jump me at the Autocrat, where I was playing with the Hawketts. It was over some stupid fight we'd had at a school dance or a football game or some humbug. Some guy came up to Izzy Koo and showed him a P38 pistol and told him, "This is for your boy Red" (he meant me; my nickname is Apache Red). A friend of Marvin's from his old neighborhood who was called Frog was there with his guys, and they were watching my back. When we took intermission and went outside, we saw Frog lying on the sidewalk in the pouring rain with a big gash in his chest. It was a sight I could never forget.

There was a lot of anger, a lot of shit that we all took out on each other. Guys were getting hassled and beat up by the cops, kept out of more than half their city by segregation, pressured by their families to be better and do better when both were really hard. Later, if my wife sometimes made me feel less than because I was out doing something stupid, I would go around by the joint (a.k.a. barroom, a.k.a. the snake pit), and if any dude got in my face, he would get the wrath from whatever my wife had said to me and wonder why.

There was a lot of pride, too. You stood up for your family, for your boys. I remember once Artie was playing with the Hawketts in a music hall in Pass Christian, Mississippi. I must have been about seventeen by then. The stage was pretty high up, and I was sitting at a table right in front of it, where a couple of ladies were also sitting. I wasn't paying any attention to them when this big, tall dude came over and started yelling at his girl. I was sitting there nodding when the guy took a swing at me. I just felt the wind from his fist, and before I could do anything my brother Artie dove off that big, tall stage onto the guy and was punching his lights out. Then Charlie picked up the mic stand with the heavy round base and hit him right between his shoulder blades. And that's when he left the place—with a guy on each side carrying him out.

Y'all didn't mess with those Neville brothers from the Calliope Projects. We couldn't just play music; we could handle any situation.

Barroom fights, nightclub fights, even street fights were not uncommon. Usually it was over a girl, but sometimes it was something that was nothing, like, "You stepped on my foot." We called this kind of fight a humbug.

One night when I was about seventeen, Melvin got into a humbug. He was going home after he dropped off his girl, who stayed in the Irish Channel, a working-class neighborhood near the river. He stopped in this sweet shop to get cigarettes and this guy kicked off some dumb shit about how Melvin stepped on his foot or something. Then one of his boys snuck up on Melvin and hit him in the face with a whiskey bottle and cut him deep. He sat out on his daddy's porch every day until it healed up, and he ended up with a scar under his eye.

Me and Melvin used to carry these small cleavers—not the big ones that the butcher uses, but smaller knives with a rectangle blade. (My mother used to say, "I can't never keep my cleavers!") We would carry them in the middle of our back, tucked into our pants.

One day a couple of months after Melvin got his scar, we were walking down the midway at Lincoln Beach when Melvin says,

"Oh, oh, up jump the devil. There's the dude I had the humbug with in the Irish Channel." He had about five of his boys with him, and it was just us two. But Melvin walked right up to him. Melvin was kind of quiet and always had this grin on his face, so you never knew what he was thinking. The dude had the same kind of shirt Melvin had on—a button-down with three-quarter-length sleeves that was the style at the time—and he said, "Hey, bro, you got a shirt just like mine." Melvin grabbed his shirt and pulled it right off him. The guy looked at me and at his boys, and asked Melvin what was wrong with him. Melvin said, "Hey, bro, you don't remember me?"

The guy said, "Bro, I don't know you."

Melvin said, "Don't you remember that place in the Irish Channel?"

And all of a sudden it dawned on him.

And then Melvin punched him in the mouth and pulled out his small cleaver and swung at him. He cut his chest, and they started running and hollering for the police. There was blood all over the midway, so we got out of there quick. We couldn't catch the Lincoln Beach bus because we knew the police would be looking for us, so we had to walk a few miles through the woods till we could reach Franklin Avenue to catch a bus home. And we couldn't go back to the beach for a long time.

There were a lot of gangs in New Orleans back then and still are today. The Hawketts sometimes played a club called the San Jacinta on Dumaine Street, and there was a window in back of the stage for the band to get out of harm's way. Sometimes some of the guys from two rival Indian krewes would get in a shootout in that club. It was exciting—I'm not gonna lie. My craving for excitement got me into a world of stupid, for sure.

One time when I was seventeen, Melvin's Uncle Willard needed new wheels for his car. When you needed a car part, you went out on the street and stole it off a car. I can't say I really thought about it; it was just what everybody did. We found the wheels we wanted and me and Melvin started stripping the car. We even took off the brake shoes. While we were at it, though, we saw lights from a police car, and we started running.

Melvin jumped a fence in the middle of the block. I kept running, and when I got to the corner the police started shooting. At that moment I do believe that God tripped me. I fell and was still slipping around on the rocks on the ground when a bullet hit the post right where my head would've been. I came up running and took a swan dive over the gate where Connie, a friend of my girl-friend, lived. I came up to her back door and said, "Connie, let me in! Some guys are after me."

Her mother came to the door, saw the flashing police lights, and said, "You better get away from here. I see what guys are after you."

We laugh about it today, but Melvin and I got caught and charged with car theft. It was my first arrest, but Melvin already had some priors; I knew they'd go lighter on me, so I was trying to take the rap off him. But his fingerprints were on the car, so there was no denying he'd been in on it.

In New Orleans, when you were being questioned you were paraded on the lineup stage, your back against a brick wall. While me and Melvin were waiting to go on the stage, they brought up this white guy named Oscar—he was a dope fiend—and started asking him questions.

"What's your name?"

"Oscar Spanier."

"Okay, what are you in here for?"

"You ought to know better than me, you got the paper out there."

"Okay, where do you live?"

"The veterans' hospital."

And they said, "What, you're a nut or something?"

And he said, "I might be."

They were trying to make fun of him, but he started talking shit to the detectives, who all were near seven feet tall.

The detectives came up on the stage and beat him till he messed himself. Then they carried him off.

When me and Melvin went up, they said, "Okay, Melvin Wright and Aaron Neville, charged with auto theft. How many other cars have y'all stolen?"

Melvin said, "This is the first one."

The detective said, "You mean your first time getting caught, huh?"

Melvin said, "No, the first one."

That went on a few times, and I could feel they were about to come up on the stage and kick our asses. So I yelled out, "Yeah, this our first time getting caught," and grabbed Melvin's arm. I told him, "Man, come on off this stage."

On your way off the stage there was always this cop standing there waiting to guff you in the stomach. He was trying to hit

Melvin, and Melvin side-stepped and the guy almost fell. I quick pulled Melvin around to the holding cells, so we missed that ass-kicking.

That kind of thing was typical. The cops loved to beat on junkies, they loved to beat on Black guys—it's hard to think of people they didn't love to beat on.

Melvin and I spent about two months in the parish prison, and then, because of his priors, he went up to Angola and I was released on bail while I waited for my sentence. While I was inside, up jumps the devil again. On our tier was the guy I shot back in the sweet shop. It turns out he just had a flesh wound—not much harm done. That was the first time I shot a gun, so I didn't know what I was doing. I was so happy that he didn't die.

His name was Dupree, and we got to be friends. One day we were sitting on the bench in the dayroom in the parish prison and he asked me, "Hey, bro, why you shot me?"

I said, "Why you hit me in my mofo mouth?"

He said, "I don't know, bro. I just didn't like the way you looked."

I said, "Well, that's why your ass got shot."

We wound up laughing about it, and I said, "I'm glad I didn't kill your ass."

When we both got out, we hung out in the streets together. Back in the day, that's how things were.

5

Chasing the Dragon

My Uncle Jolly smoked weed, and so did my brother Charles. It was no big thing; just about everybody we knew was doing it. Me and Melvin started smoking on and off in junior high, just for fun. Like I said, no big deal.

The goofballs, that was another thing. Not everyone was doing that. But a couple of kids I hung with worked as drugstore delivery guys, and they would take pills out of the pharmacy. It seemed like an adventure. So me and Melvin and Marvin decided to go for it. They called them goofballs because you'd take one and it would make you goofy. It wasn't no big thing. We were still in junior high, and we didn't do them all the time. Just every now and then.

You took whatever you could get, so we branched out into Red Devils and Christmas Trees. Nobody enticed me; it was just something I wanted to do. Anything I took, that was on me.

One day at home me and Melvin had a couple of Red Devils, and we accidentally dropped them on the floor. My dad had a dog named Pal, and he gobbled them up. We were so worried that we sat around all day, watching that dog stumbling and falling and praying he would be okay. Poppee would have killed us if something had happened to Pal. But he made it through.

I thought for sure Mommee didn't know that I was getting high, but my mom worked in a hospital and had seen a lot of stuff. Plus she had that mother way of looking all the way into you. She'd say, "You think you're cool, but who you think you're fooling? Your eyes look like two holes in a blanket."

As for heroin, I'd heard people talking about it way back in the Calliope. They called it the big stuff, or boy. (They called cocaine *girl* and marijuana *gangster*.) I knew Charles and his lady friend, Barb, were doing it. I used to see them ducking, and I knew what that meant. And I knew plenty of other people who were doing it. They seemed to be having a good time with it. I wanted to do it too. You'd sometimes hear about guys going to Angola for it, but that didn't deter me.

I was sixteen years old. I was playing gigs and making money, so I had some cash to score. And I was an inquisitive kid, always looking for the next sensation, the next experience, the next adventure. For me, heroin was just one more thing like that. It's always out there, and if you venture in the wrong vicinity, you will meet up with Mr. Jones.

So I told Charles I wanted to do heroin, and I gave him and Barb the money to score me some. They got it, but I didn't do it that day. They told me I shouldn't mess with it, and that day they talked me out of it. But I watched them do up, and I watched them nodding and scratching. It looked so good.

Plus, I was fascinated by the ritual of it all. Heroin comes in a white powder, and to shoot it you have to put it in a metal jar top or a bottle top or a spoon. Then you add just a little water. You light a match and hold the spoon over the heat so the heroin dissolves in the water. Then you get a piece of cotton and draw the liquid up into your needle through the cotton, to keep out the impurities so the needle doesn't clog and you can get every drop of the liquid. When you've got it all in the syringe, you tie off your arm to make the veins stand out so you can find them. You angle the needle so it will go in the vein and not right through it, then you stick it in and pull the plunger back. A little swirl of blood comes into the syringe—that's how you know the needle's in right. Then you push the plunger down slowly, and watch all the dope go from the syringe into your vein. It was mesmerizing.

It's not like when you get a shot at the hospital. You didn't think for a second about being sterile, or even clean. The water could be from the tap or the toilet tank or a puddle. You might pull some cotton from an old mattress or a chair or wherever. Your mind was just locked into the dope—and the ritual.

I wanted to do it, so I told them I was gonna give them money to score again for me the next day. Barb lived on Valence Street next door to my auntie and her son, so the next day I went around the corner, jumped over a fence behind Barb's house, and crawled to the back door so they wouldn't see me going there to shoot up. I felt afraid but not afraid. The adventurist in me just wanted to try it.

Barb tied my arm and found my vein easily. She said, "Damn, you got those million-dollar veins." Then she caught me (that means getting a hit). I fell in love with it instantly, and even though it made me throw up, it was the best throw-up I ever had.

I felt euphoria. It was on then. When I left, I walked straight out through the front door.

The first time you do heroin your brain is hooked in and wants it, even if your body isn't craving it yet. It's a kind of curiosity, and then it turns into a yearning that you shake off on the weekends, and then before you know it, you're in the game, running and looking for it everywhere.

After that first time, me and Melvin started scoring heroin. Marvin tried it a couple of times and it made him sick. I tell him today I'm glad it did, because it doesn't take you anyplace good.

Back then the dealers would sell heroin in capsules they called business, which was a code word, like, "Give me two or three business." You'd open the capsule and cook up the powder inside. At first we were just skin-popping on the weekends or on special occasions, like when we were going to a party. (Skin-popping is when you inject the drugs under your skin instead of right into a vein, and then they get into your blood slowly. You don't get as big a hit as when you shoot up, but the high lasts longer.) But I liked mainlining it from the jump and quickly became addicted to the whole ritual—the feeling of the needle going into my vein, seeing the blood come up in the syringe, the danger of going to score.

It was at least two years of using on and off before I really felt like I was physically hooked. I thought I was too strong-minded to fall in with Mr. Jones, but nobody is strong-minded when it comes to heroin.

By the time I was about eighteen, I wanted to shoot up more often. I would try to stay off it as much as I could, as much as the withdrawal would let me. I could go a week, until one of my junko partners would come around and whistle in a particular way, meaning he was on his way to score, and that craving just kicked in. Or somebody lit up a match and it triggered my senses about cooking up some dope. And then the jones was coming down. Marvin Gaye called the dope habit "the boy who makes slaves out of men," and he got that right.

When I got married, I was on and off for a good while, until I really got the jones for it and then it ran me. You start playing with the devil and you wind up chasing the dragon. That's what they call it when you're trying to catch the same high you felt that very first time. But you never do get that feeling again—not till you OD. That's the ultimate high.

6

My Earth Angel

A lot of things happened in my sixteenth year, but no doubt the best by far was in May, when I met Joel Francis Roux, my earth angel. I was bibbity-bopping down the street with my friend Leo Morris, the drummer, when we saw her, and I asked him to introduce us. She was going to her aunt's house to have her prom dress altered, and her aunt lived down the street from my family's house.

Right away when I saw her, I knew that she was who I wanted to be with. I guess you could say I fell in love with her at first sight. I didn't get to take her to the prom because she already had a date, but every dance after, I was the only one she danced with. I was sixteen years old; she was turning seventeen that same month.

When I first met Joel it was a no-brainer. She just took my heart. I liked everything about her—the way she walked, the way she looked. She was a little pack of dynamite. She was four feet, eleven and a half inches tall, and she wasn't afraid of nobody. Although she went to Xavier Prep Catholic High School and wore that cute Catholic schoolgirl uniform (plaid pleated skirt and black-and-white oxfords), she and her friend Naomi were kind of potty mouths. I was smitten with her—whatever that word means.

I guess she might've been drawn to me because I was sort of a bad boy. The first time we went to a drive-in movie, it was in a car I'd stolen for the occasion—which just kind of tickled her. We used to go to the movies and skating and dancing and to sock hops and parties in people's houses called waistline parties, where you paid however many pennies your waist was in inches. Me and Melvin were still at Samuel L. Green Junior High when we met, but Joel's friend Hermanese started dating Melvin, so we sometimes did things, all four of us. A few times me and Melvin picked them up in hot cars, which they loved. We never let them know we did drugs; we didn't even smoke weed around them. They had no idea.

Whenever we went to a dance together, I wouldn't let nobody else dance with her. I didn't mind the fast dances so much, but no slow dragging with Joel. If anyone got too close, I would be in their face, like "Sucker, this is my girl!" Was I jealous? Of course I was! I would've kicked anybody's ass that would try to infiltrate. She was the same way about anybody looking at me, so a couple of times I had to beat somebody up for flirting with her, and she would cuss somebody out for looking at me too much. Like I said, potty mouth. She and Naomi—those two cute Catholic high school girls would cuss someone out in a minute.

Joel's parents weren't fond of me, and her father forbade her to see me. But that just made her want to see me more. I guess the same tough-guy stuff that Joel liked is what turned off her parents. I had konked hair and two gold teeth from when Dupree punched me in my mouth, and I already had the tattoo on my face, so looking at it now, I can definitely see where they were coming from. I would've felt the same way if it was my daughter.

At first her father used to spank her for seeing me, but we would hang out together a lot anyhow. A friend of hers named Doris went to the same school and had a car, and she used to pick Joel up sometimes and bring her to see me. (Doris later married my brother Artie, and their daughter Arthel Neville is on Fox News now.) Joel would tell her parents they were going to the library, and we'd go to Lincoln Beach together. Lincoln Beach was way out in the boondocks. It was the Black beach, only in those days they called it the colored beach. (The white beach, Pontchartrain, was a lot easier to get to. But of course, we never even thought about going there.)

Joel's Aunt Ernestine (they called her Tanteen) was the only one of the grown-ups in her family who really dug me, and I was tight with her brothers, Vincent and John, and her sister, Bettina. Vinnie was heading for medical school when we met—smarts ran in her family.

Her mom was a public housing administrator and her dad was a golf pro. He was so good that he used to teach some of the white dudes at the Audubon Park golf course, where the zoo was. After we'd been dating awhile and I was allowed in the house, I would be sitting on the sofa with Joel, and when her father came home I would say, "Good evening, Mr. Roux," and he would kind of growl at me. He used to guard his sister's bar at night, so he had a .45, and he'd come in the house with his gun under one arm and his newspaper under the other. It was intimidating.

Joel had a piano at her house and could read music. Sometimes she played classical music for me, and sometimes I would play songs for her, like "In the Still of the Night" and "A Thousand Miles Away." She and Hermanese and Naomi and their friend Connie started a singing group called the Debs, and I would play piano for them. They sang at her old school, St. Joan of Arc, and they won a talent show at Lincoln Beach.

Joel came to all my gigs with the Hawketts, and she was my biggest fan. When Artie went into the navy in 1958, I became the band leader. That was the same year I started at Walter L. Cohen Senior High School.

Me and Joel were spending a lot of time together. One night she told her mother we were going to a movie, and we went to the drive-in and had sex for the first time, in the car. The guys used to brag about how many girls they had been with, but Joel was the first for me. The movie we were supposed to have seen was *Vera Cruz*. When we got home, her mother asked us what the movie was about and we said, "Well, Vera was cruising down the river in a boat." Mrs. Roux looked at us like we were crazy, and I know she didn't believe us.

A couple of months after that, Joel missed her period. I was seventeen years old and she was eighteen. I told my mother I wanted to marry her, but I was too young to do it without my parents' permission. So once again, Mommee had to sign a paper for me.

We got married on January 10, 1959, two weeks before my eighteenth birthday. My mom and dad were there, but not Joel's parents. Her friend Naomi stood up with her. We got married at my parents' house by Reverend Kennedy, a minister friend who lived in the neighborhood (his father drove the church bus). Melvin was in the penitentiary, so Marvin was my best man. After the wedding, Marvin's brother Johnny and his friend Donald went out and stole a car and got busted for auto theft.

I quit school in the eleventh grade to get married, and I guess you could say that I didn't pay close attention to much of what was being taught, with songs always going through my head. Athelgra and her friend Molly used to do my homework for me, and I don't know if that was a good thing or not. I didn't learn all the big words or figure out the math and algebra equations. My biology teacher told me that I was a waste of protoplasm.

I'm saying all of that to say this: I learned a whole lot of street smarts that got me through some really scary shit that school smarts wouldn't have. And I never felt less than because I didn't know all the big words. I believe I learned a heap more than some of the so-called scholars, and I could probably tell some of them a thing or two about life. I learned the most important things from my parents: to live by the Golden Rule, treat people as you would want to be treated, show respect to everybody, it's nice to be nice and it doesn't cost a cent. Those lessons were learned, even if I didn't always act that way.

I also took being a married man and having a family seriously. I really wanted to marry Joel, to do right for her and work hard to take care of my family. It wasn't like I felt forced to get married because she was pregnant. We were deeply in love, and I thank God for having Joel in my life—and I felt that way then, too.

Joel started at Xavier University but had to quit when she had the baby. On August 19, 1959, my son was born. We named him Aaron. When I saw him, held him, he was the sweetest thing in the world. I was a kid, but I wanted to be the dad, too. But it was a long time before I felt like I grew up.

7

Every Day

By 1959 I was married and a father. I'd heard a whole world of music and played my share of gigs. I'd also stolen quite a few cars (although I usually put them back where I found them), gotten into plenty of fights, done some heroin and some other dope, and even shot a guy. But the thing I ended up in jail for started out as a stupid little car crash a few months before I got married.

Toward the end of 1958, me and my friends Marvin, Stackolee, Lil Red, Charles, and Robert were planning to go to a picnic in Abita Springs. Robert told us he was going to borrow his daddy's Chevrolet, but we wanted to make sure we had a ride, so me and Marvin stole a Ford the night before and stashed it in our hood till morning. The next day, sure 'nuff, Robert showed up with the Chevrolet, so now we had two cars.

When we all got to the picnic, Robert said something was wrong with his daddy's car and that his daddy was going to be mad because he was supposed to be out looking for a job in that car. Then he said he was going to call the AAA to get some help. It's like he was trying to convince us it was his daddy's car.

Anyway, we took the Ford and went to the gas station to get something to fix his car with. While we were driving—yes, I was driving—these guys we knew from school, Smitty and Don, passed us, and Marvin and Stack yelled, "Get him, Aaron!" There was misty rain falling. I pushed the pedal to the metal and was flying. And all of a sudden, they stopped for a red light, and I tried the brakes and they weren't working. I knocked them almost half a block. We told the guys not to call the police, and we'd straighten it up back in New Orleans. Then we started walking back toward Abita Springs to get Robert's daddy's car, the Chevrolet.

Pretty soon two police cars from Covington, Louisiana, drove up and the cops said, "Y'all were in that Ford?"

We said, "No, we're in a Chevrolet and was seeing if we could find something to fix it." They drove off. As we were walking, we saw Robert in one of the cars that passed by. He'd caught a ride home with someone!

And before we knew it, the police came back with shotguns in their hands. They hollered, "I thought y'all said you wasn't in that car back there!" They took us to the jailhouse in Covington and locked us all in a cell.

After a while a policeman came and called me. "Hey you, the driver, come with me."

I said, "I'm not the driver. I don't even have a driver's license."

He took me outside and sat me down in the front seat of his police car. He was sitting next to me, and he had this slap jack. He kept hitting his hand with it, saying, "Now, Aaron, you gonna tell me the truth?"

I said, "I told you the truth. We weren't in the Ford, we were in the Chevrolet." Then all of a sudden, over the police radio came word that the Ford was stolen, and so was the Chevrolet. I hollered, "That's a lie. That Chevrolet is Robert's daddy's car!"

And the cop said, "No, it's a hot car."

The jig was up, but the cops wouldn't let me get back to my friends to tell them that. So they kept on lying and got the shit smacked out of them.

There were two white dudes in that little country police station for something as well, but they didn't lock them up. One of them asked us for a match, and next thing we started smelling smoke. They had set the place on fire. We were never so glad to see the New Orleans police come up there to get us.

While I was out on bond, I got busted in another hot car. Plus I was already waiting for my sentence for those wheels me and Melvin stole the year before, and something else we got up to as well (honestly, I don't even remember what). Melvin was already up in Angola, because he had some prior convictions, but this was my first. Still, I was terrified at the sentencing. My son had just been born. I wasn't scared about going to jail, but I was scared about leaving him and Joel behind.

I got six months in the parish prison. When I went before the judge, he said, "This is the first time I ever had a four-time first offender."

The sound of iron cell doors clanging shut behind me is a memory I could never forget. I heard them a few times in my life, but this time was the worst. It was just nine months after me and Joel got married and two months after my son, Aaron, was born. Joel went back to live with her parents while I was in jail, and they changed Aaron's name to Ivan.

In jail, I always met people I knew. We used to have this expression in New Orleans, "Don't sweep me with the broom," which meant bad luck and that you were going to jail. But it seemed somebody was always riding the broom on somebody, so just about everyone I knew ended up in jail sometime. I knew a bunch of guys on my tier and I wasn't scared. I was young but a big guy—bigger than most, anyway. And I was also ready for anything.

When I first went to jail, I learned how to make a shank from a razor blade melted into a toothbrush. It was a great shank, and I'm glad I never had to use it. But it was good to have, as long as the captains didn't find it when they would shake down the cells.

I remember the first night I had a dream that I broke out of prison and was partying all night all over New Orleans. In my dream, I had to get back in the jail before daylight or something really bad was gonna happen, but I couldn't get back in for anything.

When I woke up and saw the bars, I said, "Phew!" like I was happy to find myself in prison.

But I wasn't. The work was hard, and we were at it about five hours a day. There was the yank gang, which had to clean and buff the floors in the courthouse, and the paint gang, which painted stuff around the jail.

We called the guards the go-get-em squad—they would beat the hell out of anybody acting up on the tier. Once when I was in the paint gang, we were in the cage where they kept all the paint material when this guy named Dosier (who was down for murder and on his way to Angola) had some other guys on his tier hold this guy back who was supposed to be rolling out. Dosier was trying to roll out in his place so he could try to escape. But when he got to the front gate, the captain on duty recognized him and pressed the button, summoning the go-get-em squad: Captain Big Larry (a.k.a. Tombstone), Long-Nosed Johnny, and Johnny Scheme. They backed him up against a brick wall and commenced kicking his ass. He was trying to fight back, but they were too much for him. Then they brought him back on the tier and rounded up all the other guys who had helped him hold that other guy back, and they beat them all and put them in the sweat box. The sweat box was like a one-man cell but with no bars or windows, and they would put you in there with nothing on but your drawers and a bucket to do your business, and turn up the heat. I guess it could kill you if they left you in there long enough.

I missed my family like crazy. And there was no privacy. Everyone on the tier could hear everything. Sometimes in the night someone would fart, and you'd hear somebody else holler out, "Speak, oh toothless one, oh mighty jaws of wisdom, oh holy one with the bad breath."

I never let go of my music while I was inside. It was a release for me to sing, because that's what I do and who I am. Actually, in jail everybody thinks they can sing. When you got back in the dayroom after whatever work gang you were on, guys would be playing dominoes, slamming the bones down on the iron table, and in another section of the dayroom guys would be huddled up, harmonizing.

We sang mostly spirituals, because everyone gets sanctified when they go to jail. We did songs like, "Don't stay away, come on to Jesus, he will save you, oh all you dope fiends don't stay away, oh all you burglars don't stay away, oh all you car thieves." Guys would be beating on the iron table and the iron columns, and they'd at least join in on the refrain if they didn't know the words.

Like everything else in New Orleans, the prison was segregated; there were Black tiers and white tiers. Maybe occasionally you'd see a white prisoner on the way to or from the outdoor yard, but we went out at different times so it didn't happen often. There was one Black guard, and he could only say or do anything to the Black prisoners. The rest of the guards were white. The other white guy we'd see was the zu-zu man—the prisoner who came around with a cart selling candy and cigarettes and ice cream. One time the zu-zu man was none other than Dr. John. We sometimes ran together and did the dope, so when he saw me, he said, "Hey, Aaron, where you at?"

"Where you at?" is a New Orleans thing, like, "What up, bro?" I said, "I'm in here right now," and we had a laugh.

Most guys tried to stay out of fights, because the guards would take you to the hole. But there were some guys with enough stupid in them who still wanted to fight. Sometimes it was just trivial stuff, like when the *Mickey Mouse Club* would come on the TV and guys would get into fistfights saying shit like, "Annette Funicello is *my* girl." Big Peso and Chico used to fight like that.

Sometimes it was a lot more serious. There was this guy named Raymond who came on the tier bragging about what he did out in the streets, who he hung out with, and saying he was a badass heroin dealer. He used to hang around the dayroom table and watch the domino games. Then he started doing the taboo shit—borrowing money from dudes he really didn't know, like Hank and Snake, two hardened guys who were on their way back to Angola. They would loan him money and he'd say, "I'll pay you back when my pony runs on Wednesday." Well, a few Wednesdays passed, and his pony never came in, so he was in their debt. One evening when he came in from the yank gang, Snake and Hank told Raymond to get him some ready-rolled cigarettes, some ice cream and pies, and some KY jelly and bring it to his bunk that night. I guess you know what happened.

Joel didn't come to see me inside—her parents wouldn't let her—but my mother would come. We'd meet on opposite sides of a thick glass barrier with little holes in it, and you had to put your face right up to the window and almost scream to hear each other. She'd bring me some money for my commissary, and Joel was visiting her, so she'd tell me how my wife and son were doing.

There was a girl I knew from the Calliope named Teresa who used to visit sometimes too. She had become the girlfriend of this heroin dealer I knew named Jab, and just took a liking to me. She brought me money sometimes, and I asked her if she could get me some dope. So she'd come on the side of the prison by the parking lot, and there was this cement wall that was really close to the building. I would place a rock in a Bull Durham tobacco bag tied to a long string and throw it out the window and over the wall. Teresa would put some heroin in it and we'd pull it back up through the bars (that was before they put screens on all the windows). We didn't have a rig to shoot up, so we just snorted it.

While I was in jail, I got Teresa's name tattooed on my chest. I didn't think about how Joel might feel about that. I was pissed off at her for changing Aaron's name and not coming to see me—and I was still stuck in stupid at that age. So I did it. Later on her mom told her, "If I was you, I'd wait until he was sleeping and cut it out of his chest."

I was pissed because I was missing Joel and Ivan so bad. The longer the time, the more I missed them. I wrote my very first song about it; it was called "Every Day."

Every day along about one
I'm dreaming of you and my little son
Every day along about two
I'm so lonesome and so blue
Every day along about three
I'm dreaming that I'll be free.

It ended up being the first song I ever recorded. That was just about two months after I got out.

8

The Larry Williams
Experience

When I got out of jail, I couldn't wait to be with my family.
Me and Joel and Ivan stayed with my mother for a while, and Mommee and Joel got to be pretty tight. I'd sung background vocals a few
times on other people's records, but I'd been wanting to make a
record with my name on it since forever. I finally got my chance.
Larry McKinley, a New Orleans disc jockey who cofounded Minit
Records in 1959 (along with Joe Banashak), and the famous R&B
singer Larry Williams got me my first sessions. Minit Records was
the same label that recorded Ernie K-Doe and Irma Thomas, so that
meant a lot to me.

It wasn't much of a deal, really—I just got to put my voice on a
record. "Every Day" was the A-side and Allen Toussaint wrote the

B-side, "Over You." Minit had hired Allen as the label's producer, arranger, pianist, and chief songwriter. At the recording session, I played "Every Day" on the piano for Allen, and then he picked it up and worked out the arrangement right then. I learned "Over You" from Allen at the same session, just before we recorded it. There wasn't no ten or twelve takes on a recording back then—whatever you did was what you had. It wasn't like today, where they can fix things if you make a mistake. If you did harmonies, it was everyone around the same microphone.

Making a recording was amazing. To hear my voice coming back on the tape, I thought, "Oh wow, that's me!" When "Every Day" started playing on the radio, it was a big thing in New Orleans, and "Over You" was on the charts for a while.

I'd known Larry Williams since 1957, when Artie and the Hawketts went out on tour with him as his band. I was sixteen at the time—too young to go with them, Larry said—but he promised he'd be back for me. I was thrilled just thinking about it.

I had taken over the Hawketts in 1958 when Artie went into the navy. That was on hold while I was in prison, but after I got out in 1960, I ended up headlining the band for a while. And just like he promised, Larry took me out on the road with him that year after my record came out, in a show with Jackie Wilson, the Drifters, the Coasters, the Flamingos, the Isley Brothers, and some other groups. That's when I got my first taste of the Larry Williams experience.

Larry'd had some big hits in the '50s, starting with "Short Fat Fannie," which got to number one in the summer of 1957. "Bony Maroney," "Dizzy, Miss Lizzy," "Bad Boy," and "She Said Yeah" were all his too. He got arrested in New Jersey in 1959 on drug and gun charges, so we might have been in jail at about the same time. Anyway, his record label dropped him, so when he got out he put together his own touring show. It was usually six acts, and we'd sing five songs each. Tickets were five dollars. Larry had his own band with him, and I sang with them too, but the rest of the singers were backed by a local house band. There wasn't much rehearsal time, but we were all singing our hits, so the local guys knew our songs.

Actually, Jackie Wilson missed a couple of gigs right after I joined the tour. They'd been playing the Auditorium in New Orleans. Larry Williams had second billing under Jackie, so he'd sing a couple of numbers and then come out into the audience and stir the crowd up. When he came off of the stage, though, this Black cop named Perry White came up, put his billy club in Larry's face, and told him to get back on the stage. That's when Jackie came out and tried to explain that it was a part of Larry's act. The cop got stupid and pushed Jackie and swung at him. Jackie was once a boxer, so he blocked the lick and hit the cop. That's when all these police ran over there and popped Jackie's head open, and he had to miss a couple of shows. He wore a bandage on his head for a few shows after he joined us.

I was nineteen when I went out on tour, just a kid, and it was the first time I was far from home. I think the farthest away I'd ever been was Mississippi. Now I was like a little kid going on an adventure. I always craved the action, and this was the real deal. Larry and I were about the same size (I told you I was a big kid), so he gave me some of his suits to wear onstage, and we were off.

We sang six shows a day in some places, and I made good money, plus a per diem. And I got to sing and to travel around the country. I loved it. It was one of the most exciting times of my young life, being out on the road and singing for audiences in big theaters. And I was onstage with some of my idols.

Everyone was responsible for getting to the gigs on their own, but I used to ride with Larry and his wife and Lee Tillman, who was Larry's valet, in his powder-blue Lincoln Continental. I remember how exciting it was to be with Larry and Lee in that big fancy car. We'd drive all day, find a hotel or a guesthouse where Black people could stay, get something to eat, go to the gig, sometimes go to a party after, then back to the hotel and go to bed. And the same the next day. Nothing fancy; you just catch what you can on the road.

We played a series of clubs and theaters that were known as the Chitlin Circuit. The little ones might be just a shabby bar (a.k.a. a jook joint) or even a hall in a church, but there were also some really nice clubs and high-end theaters like Atlanta's Royal Peacock, Baltimore's Royal Theater, Chicago's Regal Theater, Detroit's Paradise Theatre, Harlem's Apollo Theater, and Washington DC's Howard and Lincoln Theaters—all of which we played. A lot of them were owned or at least run by Black people, and the audiences were all Black in the South—although they got more mixed as you went farther north.

Traveling through the segregated South in 1960 was no joke. You always had to be on your Ps and Qs, and sometimes even that didn't matter. One time Larry's tires squealed as we pulled into a gas station in Alabama. The local sheriff ran the gas station, and he came out and said Larry was speeding. He asked for ID from everyone in the car, and Larry ended up having to pay a fine when all he did was stop to get some gas. Larry also had a sticker on his car that said "I stop for blondes," and that was just asking for trouble.

We all knew about Jesse Belvin, who had a number two hit with "Dream Girl" (one of my favorites; later I recorded one of his songs, called "Goodnight My Love"). On February 2, 1960, he played a gig with Sam Cooke, Jackie Wilson, and Marv Johnson that was the first integrated concert ever in Little Rock, Arkansas. The concert was stopped twice when white people in the audience shouted out racist insults and told the white teenagers, who were there to hear that great music, to get out. Someone slashed Jesse's tires, and he and his wife were killed when his car crashed.

And just a couple of years later, in 1963, Sugar Boy Crawford, the New Orleans musician who wrote "Iko Iko," was driving to a show in northern Louisiana when he was stopped by the police, pulled out of his car, and pistol-whipped. He said later that the police saw a Black man at the wheel of a flashy new car and actually set up a roadblock to stop him. He ended up in a coma with a metal plate in his skull and had to learn how to walk, talk, and play the piano all over again.

These kinds of things happened all the time, and even though they usually didn't end up in the newspapers, we knew about them. So once I got to where we were going, I sometimes didn't leave the hotel until it was time to go to the gig.

Still, it was a big adventure for me. This was in the days long before GPS, so you had to read road maps. It wasn't that easy with all the little roads and highways, and I remember once when Larry asked me to drive while he slept, I wound up going two hundred miles out of the way. It's a good thing we didn't have a gig that night! We laughed about it, but Larry didn't let me drive anymore.

We were out on the road for about two months, playing maybe two or three days in each place. Sometimes if the crowds were really big, we'd be held over an extra day or two. But mostly we just kept moving.

Sometimes Larry would double-book himself—two gigs on the same night—and then I'd wear his suit and go do one of the gigs as Larry. When Artie toured with Larry, he did the same. This was back before singers were on TV, so people didn't always know what you looked like, and it happened all the time. There was a booking agent in New Orleans named Percy Stovall who used to send a guy named Eldridge out as different singers. He would say, "Hey, Eldridge, put on those dark glasses; you're gonna be Ray Charles tonight," or, "Hey, Eldridge, you're gonna be Ernie K-Doe." Everybody on the circuit knew Stovall. There were all kinds of people going out as me, too. There was a guy I went to school with named Chester, and people said that we favored each other. One time when my brother Charlie was in Florida, he saw a poster saying that Aaron Neville was gonna be playing at this club. Charlie went over there and busted him, and Chester pleaded with him, "Don't bust me. I'll split the money with you."

When I was out with Larry, I saw plenty of stuff I'd never seen before. One time we had a gig at a Black club in Federalsburg, Maryland, and they had some rowdy people in there. Larry had a friend with him from New Orleans named Sonny, who had a pistol. The band members had their girls with them, and this dude came over and started messing with the girls. Sonny told him to back off, and the dude swung at Sonny, so Sonny hit him with the gun. His people came in and were going to jump Sonny, so Sonny shot one of them—which gave us a chance to make it out of there. We got in Larry's Lincoln and took off down the highway with cars following us, guys shooting at us out the window. Me and Lee Tillman had glass all in our hair from a shotgun breaking the back window, but we left them in the dust. That was one Larry Williams experience. Maybe it sounds crazy, but I loved the excitement. It was like being in a movie.

Me and Lee used to share a hotel room, and we got to be great friends. Lee was also a singer, and we'd harmonize together in the room. We wrote a song called "Have Gun Will Travel," based on the TV Western. When we were in Lancaster, Pennsylvania, we met these two Quaker girls who were twins and hung out with them for a few days. We didn't do anything but kiss. They thought I couldn't tell them apart and would try and trick me. Actually, I could, but I played along and wound up kissing them both.

The movie *Psycho* came out that year, and me and Lee went to see it. I had no idea what "psycho" meant—I just wanted to go to the movies. There was this lady sitting behind us who had bought popcorn, a hotdog, and fries. When the shower scene came on she got so scared that she left her stuff on the seat and just ran out of the theater. So me and Lee ate all her food and didn't have to buy anything.

When we were in Washington, DC, Larry didn't want to pay the hotel bill. So Lee and me grabbed our suitcases and climbed down the drainpipe. I didn't think anything of it—that was just part of the Larry Williams experience.

I was still a kid, so I thought all that shit was cool. It was actually a really great time on the road with Larry. He'd take me to parties where there were lots of drugs and lots of girls. I didn't mess around with any girls while I was out there—I was really shy, and also married—but it made me feel good about myself just to be treated like one of the singers in the group.

One of the highlights of that tour was being with all the famous people Larry knew. I used to hang with Billy Guy of the Coasters. We'd smoke weed together and stand out in front of the theater and girl-watch. He called me *Aaaaaaron*; he was a funny dude. So was Speedo (a.k.a. Earl Carroll) from the Cadillacs. I once met Della Reese at a party, and she was smitten with me.

Later, when we were in New York, we visited Ray Charles—another friend of Larry's—in his hotel room. I was a big-time fan and had sung some of his songs with the Hawketts. He was there with David Newman (a.k.a. Fathead), his sax player. Ray told me he really liked my record "Over You," which was going up the charts then. Man, that felt great!

Fathead had scored some heroin, and I watched them put the biggest clump of heroin I'd ever seen in a mayonnaise jar top and get ready to shoot up. They asked me what my shot was (meaning how much I usually shot up), and I said, "I'll put some water on y'all's cotton." If I had asked for anything more, I would've OD'd. That was some serious shit. I remember being amazed that although Ray was blind, he didn't need any help shooting up. He'd just tie off, slap his arm, and find his own vein by pure feel.

While we were in New York, we went backstage at the Apollo and watched Patti LaBelle and the Bluebells singing "Somewhere Over the Rainbow." Patti was killing it. Later we went to this party where they had some of everything. I smoked some weed and it was good. I snorted some coke and I was lit. Larry scored a lot of drugs at the party—heroin, cocaine, weed—and stashed it all in an overnight case. Weed always makes me goofy, and I started laughing because everyone was looking funny to me, and the lady who gave the party kept smiling at me in this weird way. I told Larry that I was ready to get out of there, so he gave me the overnight case and asked me to take it back to our hotel.

The hotel we were staying in was across the street from the party, so I walked across the street and sat down on the stoop of the building—and nodded out. When I came out of my nod there was a policeman standing there. The police used to walk around the hotels sniffing for weed, but I wasn't smoking then, just sleeping. He said good morning. I said good morning. Then he walked up the stairs with me. And I walked up to my room with the overnight case. If that policeman had had an inkling of what I had in the overnight case—phew! It was just another part of the Larry Williams experience.

9

The Burglary Booking Agent

After I came back from my road trip adventure with Larry Williams in 1960, I started gigging just about every weekend and recording regularly for Minit Records. Allen Toussaint was usually my producer, and he wrote a lot of songs for me, including "I'm Waitin' at the Station," "Just a Little Love," and "How Could I Help But Love You." He used his mother's maiden name as a pseudonym (a tax thing, I think—who knows?), and everyone thought those songs were written by my mother because her name was Naomi Neville. Allen might possibly have been kin to us in some way; I don't really know.

Despite recording all the time, I wasn't making any money at it. Which was typical at the time. They'd pay you a few hundred dollars at the recording session, and then you'd never see another dime from your records, no matter how much they got played on the radio or how many copies were sold. I had a family to support, so I took what work I could find on the docks unloading ships, or painting houses, or driving a truck. Joel was working as a teacher's helper with one of her aunts, and as a waitress at her Aunt Tanteen's bar at the time, but I was still the breadwinner.

It was hard, physical work, and I don't have anything against hard work, but it wasn't what I wanted to be doing. My life was basically hustling for work, hustling for gigs, hustling for dope—not the life I wanted.

The New Orleans police added what we call the lagniappe by hauling me and my friends in repeatedly for nothing at all. They'd come into the Black neighborhoods and call us "boy" and shit like that, and it was hard to take. It was regular practice for them to harass and arrest Black men, and especially Black men they knew were in the drug game. We'd always get released, but every time they picked us up it was an automatic seventy-two hours in a precinct holding cell. They didn't have to charge you with anything. And every time a shift changed, they'd bring you to a lineup. If you looked kind of like someone they were looking for, you got charges put on you—that happened to a lot of guys.

I remember one night in 1962 me, Melvin, and our friend Vernon were standing in front of the pool hall at the Bumble Bee bar just shooting the shit when the police pulled up and started to harass us. The police decided to arrest me and Vernon for vagrancy—we were the only ones out there that had jobs, so go figure—but they let

Melvin go. He'd just come home from Angola, so Melvin got lucky that night. We lived right down the street, and he went and told Joel. She came down there and started giving the police a piece of her mind. "Y'all aren't taking my husband to jail; he has a job," she yelled.

One of the cops said to her, "Look, lady, you better go home."

"I'm not going nowhere till you let my husband go."

They went back and forth like that until Joel ended up in the police car too, and they took her along with me and Vernon to the precinct.

They stuck us in a cell and locked Joel in the walk-around. Her Aunt Tanteen came and got her out that night, but me and Vernon had to stay in for seventy-two hours "pending an investigation." What were they investigating for three days? We were picked up for vagrancy—which means hanging around without a home or a job. We both had addresses and places we worked. I lived a few blocks away, and my wife was standing there yelling at them!

Things like that happened so often that we just got used to it. There was a lot wrong with this kind of shit, but one of the things was that when you had a job, you suddenly had to miss three days of work, so how were you supposed to keep that job? It became a crushing cycle.

In May 1962 my second son was born, and we named him Aaron. The name stuck this time (although later he started calling himself Fred). I loved my family, and I absolutely wanted to take care of them. But I wanted to do it by singing. Even though I kept gigging and recording, my career was going nowhere. Sometimes

I'd be down in the hole of a ship, singing, and it sounded so good in those big, hollow spaces. Guys would tell me I ought to be on the radio, and I always said, "I will be." But it was hard waiting for that to happen.

Meanwhile, Larry Williams was out in Los Angeles then. Back when we were on the road together, he said he was tired of being pimped by record companies and booking agents and that he was going to go back to LA to start doing his own pimping. In 1962, when I was twenty-one, Larry sent for me to come join him. He said he was going to manage me and promised he'd get me recorded in LA on a big label with real distribution, and gigs at the fancy clubs there. Larry seemed larger than life to me at the time, but actually his career was dwindling, and he was just out of prison on another drug charge. He was still living a fancy life, but he paid for it by booking high-priced hookers and burglaries.

Larry picked me up from the airport in a brand-new black Cadillac Eldorado. In LA, pimps drove Cadillac Eldorados, and I actually heard a disc jockey on a radio station out there make a joke, "Wow! There goes a white guy in an Eldorado!"

On the way to Larry's house from the airport, he made a stop at a motel. I stayed in the car, but I could hear him dealing with his client (a.k.a. a prostitute). Eventually the police pulled up behind his car and a cop got out and came to my window on the passenger side. He must have recognized Larry's car, because he said, "Hi, what are you, a pimp? A stickup man? A burglar?"

I said, "No, I'm a singer."

He said, "Well, what are you doing with Mr. Williams?"

I said, "He's my manager."

The cop laughed and said, "Well, they call me Red. I work out of the Wilshire District and I'll see you over there." Then he left.

I told Larry about it when he came out, and he said, "Them's jive-ass poot butts, jealous of a Black man in a Cadillac." But sure enough, it wasn't long before me and Larry were stopped—back in the day they routinely stopped guys they knew were pimps—and ended up at the Wilshire District police station.

Red said, "I told you I'd be seeing you again."

In fact, I was meeting up with the police a lot. Once they picked us up along with Larry's poodle, Shanel. The policeman said, "How do you interrogate a poodle?"

I went to California because I wanted to sing, and I thought that's where it was going to happen for me. This was the land of movie stars and big producers and people arriving with nothing and ending up with a whole lot of something. Larry promised me I'd end up that way too. Me, Larry, Johnny "Guitar" Watson, and Etta James did a few gigs at the 5-4 Ballroom (a really famous jazz and blues club in South Central LA), but we didn't gig that often. Larry did have the connections to get me a recording deal, but Minit Records wouldn't let me out of my contract, so that never happened. I learned the hard way a couple of times in my career that people make promises they do not keep; their lawyer tells you it will all be okay, but then it's not. It's a part of the music business that everyone who is in it has had to taste.

Meanwhile, I was living with Larry and his wife, and he was getting me dope as well. I had to earn my keep. Larry kept telling me that the whores wanted to give me that whore money, but I told him I wasn't no pimp. I had a wife, a mother, and a sister, and I couldn't do that.

So Larry told me he knew a different kind of booking agent—one who booked burglaries and stickups. The booking agent would set up the scores and we would go and steal the merchandise—high-end stuff, mostly men's suits—and bring it to a few rooms they rented at the Starlighter Motel, right off the freeway. All we had to do was drop off the stuff and get our money. Someone else came in later to handle the sales. They would fill about three rooms full of suits—sometimes they would even bring in mannequins—and people would come in to buy them.

I did not like the idea. My stomach went right into convulsions, so before I would do any of it, I had to get really high on coke and heroin to get up enough nerve. That's the only way I could do shit like that; the heroin gives you a sort of false courage.

I was part of a little crew. Sometimes we would park the car on the freeway and watch when the security guards made their rounds. Then we would run off the freeway, break a store window, and snatch things like jewelry right out of the window. One night, the mayor of one of those little towns outside of LA set up his own store to be burglarized so he could get an insurance payoff. He had taken half the stuff out before we got there, but there was still a big load left for us to take to the Starlighter Motel.

We got a lot of money from those jobs, so we didn't have to do them too often—maybe once a month or so. But my nerves were being shattered. I would have to do heroin before and after every

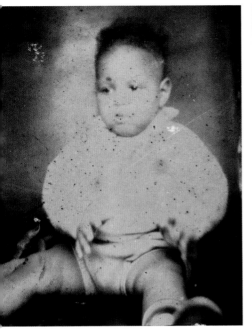

hat's me sometime in my first year. This big aby came out of my mother knees first.

A school picture from St. Monica's. That's the real innocence.

This is my eighth-grade graduation picture from St. Monica's. Not as innocent.

I'm holding my little sister Cookie in front of our house in the Calliope Project. This was about 1953, and I was twelve. Cookie wasn't with us long enough, but she stayed in our hearts.

Mommee—Amelia Landry Neville—the sweetest woman in the world, and my first angel.

My second angel, Joel Roux Neville, at her high school graduation. That's the year I met her, and you can see why I fell in love—and why her daddy didn't want her with me.

Me and my little sister, Athelgra, my third angel. I could do no wrong in her eyes.

A happy time with Joel hanging on my strong arm.

My friend George Green took this picture for me in the 1970s. I had my hair natural by then, so a brick would have bounced off my hair.

was giving Marvin a konk. Today he tells me he's going to call a lawyer to sue me for making him lose his hair.

Moleface and Melvin, my great friend and brother. We were friends since we were about six years old. You seen one, you seen them both.

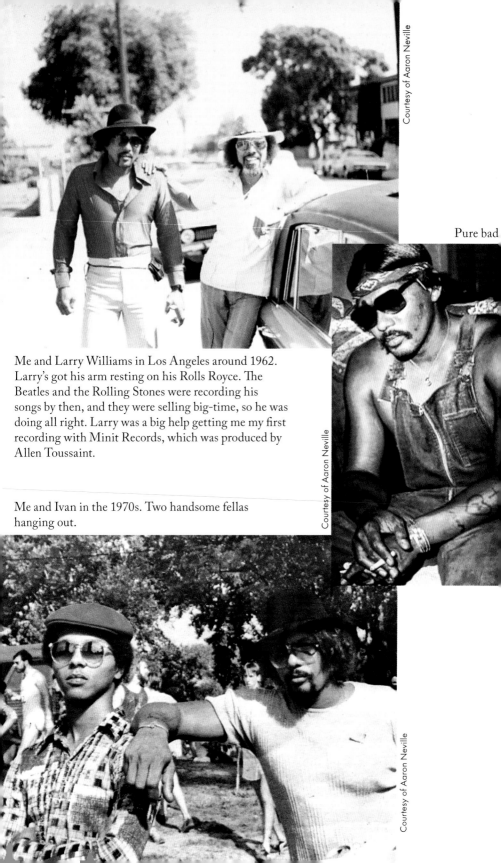

Pure bad

Me and Larry Williams in Los Angeles around 1962. Larry's got his arm resting on his Rolls Royce. The Beatles and the Rolling Stones were recording his songs by then, and they were selling big-time, so he was doing all right. Larry was a big help getting me my first recording with Minit Records, which was produced by Allen Toussaint.

Me and Ivan in the 1970s. Two handsome fellas hanging out.

My publicity picture from 1966 for *Tell It Like It Is*. My manager, Joe Jones, arranged this photo shoot. I was in a tuxedo made just for me, and I was so high, both physically and emotionally.

The Hawketts around 1958. That's me on the left. Behind me (you can't hardly hardly see him) is George French on bass. My brother Charlie the Horn Man is next to me, and Kidd Jordan is on baritone sax.

The Aaron Neville Quintet on *The Today Show*. From left to right: Charlie the Horn Man, David Johnson (bass and vocals), me, Earl Smith Jr. (drums and vocals), Michael Goods (keyboards and vocals), and Shane Theriot (stooping down, guitar and vocals). A badass band.

Big Chief Jolly (a.k.a. Geoge Landry) in his full regalia. He was a real influence on all of us. If it wasn't for him getting us all together, there wouldn't have been the Neville Brothers.

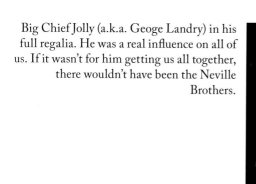

We loved the Indian parades at Mardi Gras. This is in 1978. That's me with the tambourine and the funky Afro. Next to me was Jason, who was seven; then a friend of Cyril's; then Big Chief Jolly in his full regalia; and next to him George Porter of the Meters.

The Wild Tchoupitoulas at Jazz Fest in 1977. That was the beginning of it all.

The Neville bros and the Wild Tchoupitoulas at Jazz Fest 1447/9 Michael P. Smith 1977

e and Artie with Mayor Dutch Morial
t a 1982 performance. The good mayor
helped me put together the Uptown
Youth Center.

...rles, Art, Cyril, Aaron, & Ivan   183/16   Michael P. Smith, 1980

e Brothers plus one, from
30. That's Charles on the left,
n Art, Cyril (stooping),
n, and me. It's a great photo.

Charlie, Izzy Koo (a.k.a.
Isacher Gordon), and me in
the early 1980s. Izzy Koo and
Artie are the ones who taught
me how to harmonize.

I got clean in 1981, and suddenly I had a lot more energy. Here I am getting myself on track, giving back to the community, and helping a lot of kids in the neighborhood.

Doing my thing. This was probably some time in the late 1980s. You can see that I was working out with my trainer in New Orleans, Tazzie Colomb. She is a great trainer, and her arms were bigger than mine.

job. Honestly, the whole time I was saying to myself, "Lord, get me out of this. Send me back home, please." I had come to LA to help my career take off, and somehow I kept thinking I could still make a record. Sometimes when you have a big dream, you want it so bad and you cling to it so tight that you do some very stupid things.

One night in the summer of 1963, we were going to rob this men's clothing store on Sunset Boulevard. I was with Larry on that job. The men's store had a burglar alarm, so the guys with us popped the lock on the women's store next door that didn't have an alarm and went through the wall with a pickax and sledgehammers. Then they made a hole big enough for someone to come through with an armload of suits. The booking agent had rented us this step-in van with a sliding door, which we parked in the alley behind the store.

While we were in the store, a guy thought someone had seen us, so everyone ran out and scattered in different directions. Me and this guy named Steve went and sat on a bench on Sunset at the bus stop. Later, Steve went to see what was going down. It looked like everything was okay, so Steve went back in the store to see if the coast was clear. After he had been gone for a bit, I decided to go and see what was happening, so I went back through the alley. As I was approaching the step-in van I heard some voices, so I eased the van door open, crawled in, and slid it shut.

I was so high; I had done heroin and smoked weed, and the weed made me goofy. I could hear someone getting closer to the van, and then a man said, "Hey, someone's in the store." Then his tone changed and he yelled, "Who are you and what are you doing in the store?"

I heard Larry say, "Man, leave us alone, we're cleaning up," and the lady said, "I didn't hire anyone to clean up my store."

My imagination was going wild. I was picturing Larry and them looking at each other and I was rolling back and forth in the back of the van—the weed had me laughing my head off. It was so crazy; the adrenaline was heavy.

Larry came out of the store first and the guy grabbed him. Larry punched him, knocking him down, and then the lady started screaming. Everybody ran off in different directions. I was trying my best to slide that van door open to get out and run away, but it just wouldn't open, no matter what I did. Not until the alley filled up with people, including the sheriff of Hollywood. That's when the door just slid right open. To this day, I believe God locked that sliding door, keeping me in the van, so I could stop what I was doing—because as soon as the sheriff came up, the door slid open like it was greased. I just sat on the running board, lit a cigarette, and said, "Thank you, Jesus." I was so relieved.

The sheriff said to me, "What's happening?"

And I said, "I guess I'm busted." I think I was actually smiling.

Larry and the other guys got away, and the police started combing the area for them. I fell asleep in the back seat of the police car with my hands cuffed behind my back so tight that even now, almost sixty years later, I still have to click my thumb back and forth every morning to get it working right. About three in the morning I raised my head up and saw Larry drive by in his car with his wife; he'd called her to come pick him up after he had ran through the

Hollywood Hills. His konked hair was shining all over his head as he looked at me. I nodded and they went on.

The police brought me to the precinct and booked me on two counts of second-degree burglary. They asked me who was with me. I gave them some phony names, and they knew I was lying. One cop said, "I'm gonna send your ass to San Quentin."

I said, "I guess I have to go. I told you the truth."

Nobody else ever got caught for that break-in—it was all on me. That was my third and last burglary.

Before I tell you the rest of this story, let me tell you about that bench on Sunset Boulevard me and Steve sat on that night. One day about twenty-five years later, me and my son Ivan were driving down Sunset and passed by that same bench, and Ivan said it was the bench he had picked out in case he was ever homeless. He even named his music publishing company Sunset Bench after it. Then I told him about my adventure, when I sat on that bench the night of the burglary.

Anyway, Larry got me out on bond and got me a lawyer. He told me they had run the shit outta him in the Hollywood Hills, but he got away when he jumped over a fence and wound up in somebody's swimming pool. That's why his konk was all over his head when he drove by, all innocent like, to see how it turned out. About a month later I went to trial and was found guilty. They gave me a month to come back to court for sentencing, so I went home to New Orleans to spend that time with my family.

A few years earlier, my mother had turned me on to St. Jude, the patron saint of lost cases, and I guess I fit the bill. Me and my mother

and Joel started going to Our Lady of Guadeloupe, on the corner of
North Rampart Street and Conti, which is where they put up the
International Shrine of St. Jude in the 1930s, after some parish-
ioners there who prayed to St. Jude had their prayers answered. The
priests there say regular novenas to St. Jude, and there's a relic from
him. We started going and asking him to help me.

We asked Jesus, too. On Ursulines Avenue in the Treme neighborhood is the St. Ann's Shrine. It was built in 1902 as a copy of the
grotto at Lourdes, in France, and it's known for the miraculous
powers of the spring water there. In the middle is a long staircase
that's a copy of the Holy Stairs in Rome, and you go up the steps on
your knees, praying on each step. At the top, in the open air, is a
life-size statue of Jesus on the cross with Mary and John standing
on either side and Mary Magdalene kneeling down between them.
We three did a lot of praying in both places that month. Plus my
mother and Joel wrote letters to the court, saying that I was really a
good man with a family.

And then I had to go back to LA.

I will admit that I was plenty scared. But if I didn't go back, I'd
be on the run for the rest of my life. I couldn't be with my family and
I couldn't sing. So I had to go there and take my issue.

The night before my sentencing, Larry arranged for me to spend
the night with two nineteen-year-old girls named Arty and Kim.
One had dark skin and the other had really light skin, and I remember calling them chocolate and vanilla. I smoked weed and snorted
some coke and heroin, so whatever happened that night is kind of
blurry. I remember how we started but I don't remember how we

finished. I guess I was trying to get as high as I could so it would last till I got to jail.

They looked like two innocent girls from down South who had come up to LA to seek their fortune. The pimps would tell them, "Hey, baby, I'm gonna make you a star," which was the biggest lie ever told because they were just going to use them. When I was doing my time, I prayed for Arty and Kim. I mean, they could've been anyone's little sisters; they just got caught up in that web. And I guess we had something in common too. All three of us came to LA with a dream of doing something really big and beautiful, and we all got trapped in something small and ugly.

When I went to the court the next day for sentencing, I had my St. Jude medal Mommee had given me. My lawyer had spoken with Judge Brand, who said he would go light on me after reading the letters from my mother and Joel. But when I got to court, Judge Brand was on vacation. This other judge was on the bench and he was giving out time like ice water—five to life, one to fourteen, like that. I was sitting in the back of the court thinking about running out of there, but I said to myself, "If you run, you won't be able to sing." No matter what kind of trouble I got myself into, I always had something I wanted more. I was still stuck in stupid, but I think that dream saved me from a lot worse. I decided I had to take my time.

When it was my turn to stand in front of the judge, I felt like I was two feet tall and the judge was a giant. He looked at me and said, "You were found guilty on two counts of second-degree burglary. I sentence you to what the law prescribes, which is one to fourteen years in San Quentin." My legs turned to butter. Then he said, "But . . . ," and when he said that, I was holding on to a piece of kite string for dear life. My lawyer had to hold me up. "But I suspend that sentence and place you on a three-year probation, provided you do the first year for the county."

I said, "Thank you, Your Honor, and thank you, God and St. Jude, the patron saint of the impossible."

10

Mr. 016955

After my sentencing, I spent about a week in the Los Angeles County Jail. They called it the Glass House because the windows were made of this special extra-thick glass so they didn't have bars on them.

The day I got there, about twenty guys were being booked in. While we were walking between the cell blocks, some guy in one of the blocks yelled, "Take that fucking hat off!" and some of the older guys who were wearing hats quickly snatched them off.

I yelled back at him, "Tell your mama to take that fucking hat off!" He shut up. I didn't have a hat on, but that's always been my reaction to bullies—to let them know that I was a man amongst men and would bring it to anyone who came in my face with any of that kind of shit.

When I was being transported to the Glass House, they cuffed me to this Black guy from Houston, Texas, named Robert. He was kind of tall, walked like he was a cowboy or something, and had a chip on his shoulder from the get-go. Robert was walking around like he was the baddest lion in the jungle; he seemed like he wanted to challenge everyone he came across. I would tell him, "Hey, Robert, you ought to chill with that bully attitude." He didn't take my advice.

At the Glass House they asked me if I wanted to do my time inside or outside. That was a no-brainer—I didn't like the sound of iron cell doors closing behind me. So I said I'd like to do it outside. I ended up at Wayside Honor Rancho, which was in Castaic, California, up near Pasadena—with Robert cuffed to me again.

The "Honor" part meant we weren't locked up in cells. Instead, it was built like a small town, with two rows of barracks, fifty on each side, and about fifty guys living in each barracks building. In the middle was the chow hall, library, hospital, and main office. There were a couple of baseball diamonds and football fields, and there was even a small dairy farm. Unlike the segregated prisons in Louisiana, this place had people from all walks of life and all nationalities— Black, white, Latino, Asian. It was actually pretty exciting.

At the south end, where me and Robert were, was a firefighting training camp, where you learned how to fight forest fires in LA County. I took the training seriously and learned everything I could so I wouldn't wind up getting hurt. I could take a shovel full of dirt and flip it just right to put out a flame high up on a tree branch. I was proud of that skill. I learned how to use a Pulaski (a special firefighting tool with an ax on one side of the head and an adze on the other) and how to set a back fire, where you start a fire on the inside edge of a fire line to cut off the fuel and stop the fire from going any farther. The work was physically hard and plenty dangerous, but I learned really fast and got pretty good at it.

After about a month of training, we were assigned to a firefighting camp, and we lucked out and got Camp 18. That used to be officers' barracks, and it was made out of bricks and was state-of-the-art (a lot of the other barracks were like wooden shacks). It had a good cafeteria and a great gym, and I started working out with the weights. That was my first time getting into body building, and I was geeked. I got up to benching 270 pounds, and after about a month I was looking like the Hulk. It felt so good to be healthy and drug-free. The weight room became my drug. I was twenty-two years old and happy to be there.

My boy Robert seemed like he didn't like nobody, and would walk around the compound like he was in Dodge City or something. He would tell guys, "Hey, get outta my way," and expected them to just move aside. They'd look at him like he was crazy. Once he messed with this Japanese guy who turned him upside down, but that didn't deter Robert. He still thought he was the barracks bully.

Finally, Robert tried to take some food from this little white guy in the chow hall, and the guy pressed him up against the wall with some kind of judo move. That was the last I saw of Robert or that little white dude, because when you had a fight in Camp 18 you went to the hole (a.k.a. Siberia). Nobody wanted to go to Siberia, but

Robert and the other guy ended up there. Things were a lot more peaceful after that.

The sergeant over our compound was a nice guy with a jovial kind of face; he was always smiling. He knew how to take the measure of every man he met, and I guess he could see into my heart, because he took a liking to me. He asked me once, "Aaron, what are you doing in a place like this? You don't seem the type."

I said, "I did some stupid shit, so here I am, paying my debt." My number, sewn onto the pocket of my shirt, was 016955, and he used to call me that—Mr. 016955.

Camp 18 was seven thousand feet up in the Los Angeles National Forest (sometimes we'd be up above the clouds), and there were quite a few fires there up on Mount Wilson. (Although they are nothing like the infernos you see in California now. They look like they're on steroids compared to the fires we fought.) When we went out on a fire call we rode in the back of a truck with canvas over the top, holding our gear. We had a few harrowing moments riding in those trucks on those skimpy little roads. A couple of times we would see the back wheels actually sliding off the road and all we could do was pray, but our sergeant was an excellent driver and maneuvered us out of danger. We would just suck in our breath and say, "Whew!" It was dangerous work, but a thousand times better than being locked in a cell.

One time we almost got trapped in a box canyon, with the Santa Ana winds making the fire climb the mountain faster than a man could move. You could feel the fire blocks away and hear the trees exploding. It sounded like a war. I prayed the whole time. We had to be pulled out of there in a helicopter.

It was scary, but exciting at the same time. Once I remember hearing people saying, "Thank God, here come the boys to save us!" That was a great feeling. I even thought of being a firefighter for a while, but it wasn't a good idea with me having asthma. And of course, then I couldn't be a singer—just a singing fireman.

Larry sent me money in my commissary account, and so did Joel and my mother. Plus we were paid fifty cents a day. I actually had all the money I needed. I watched myself get really healthy, and I felt like that was where I was supposed to be at that time. I guess it was a continuation of my blessings from God and St. Jude.

I was tight with two Chicano guys, John and Pedro. We would hit the gym together and spot each other, and I learned a lot about lifting from them. John was kind of a hothead, and it seemed like I was the only one who could talk to him when he was pissed off. The sergeant that was over his crew kept riding John for no reason we could see, other than that they didn't like each other. One day we were out on the grade digging up old burned tree stumps and the sergeant did something to piss John off. John got fed up and pinned him up against the truck. Pedro came and found me and said, "Hey, Aaron, *mi amigo*, come talk to John before he does something stupid."

I told John to lighten up on the sergeant because he didn't have that much more time to go and he didn't want to let that asshole make him spend the rest of it in Siberia. John let up, but he had put the fear in his sergeant. The sergeant didn't press charges against him, and he showed a little more respect to John after that.

John and Pedro also liked to sing. In fact, there were a few cats in there who were thugs on the street but liked to sing in the barracks. So we put together a doo-wop harmony group and would practice in the shower, like I did in junior high and high school, because it had those great acoustics. We harmonized just like the Flamingos and the Moonglows. We were so good that the Camp 18 sergeant had us put on a concert for the whole camp. Everybody thought they could sing, so they all wanted to be involved. But we only invited the guys who could really sing.

We were totally cut off from the world up there, seven thousand feet in the air. I remember one afternoon in November 1963, we were out digging up old burned tree stumps and acting like kids, playing with scorpions, potato bugs, and centipedes. We had a glass jar we would put them in and see who was the toughest (hands down, the scorpion). Suddenly the sergeant told us we were going back to camp and that President Kennedy had been assassinated. It was a sad day, and I felt bad because I really dug the president.

In December of that year the Beatles' first record came out in the United States, and we didn't even know who they were. I remember hearing it on the radio in the captain's office, though—"I Wanna Hold Your Hand"—and it kept me awake all night with that tune going through my head. I said, "That's gonna be a big hit," and sure 'nuff, it was.

We were cut off in another way too. We were allowed visitors, but the camp was so remote that a lot of guys didn't get any. I certainly didn't, with my family all the way in New Orleans. Joel and I wrote to each other all the time, but it was hard not getting to see anyone from the outside. I got to be friends with a guy named Allen from Mending, Louisiana. His family had moved to Los Angeles, and they came to visit him regularly. When they did, his mother would say she was my visitor and call me out to the picnic benches. It was so nice to sit with his family and talk. His mother would ask me, "What is a nice young man like you doing in here?" I guess I looked innocent.

One of my jobs used to be to buff the floors in the captain's office. I had used the buffing machine when I was working on the yank gang in the courthouse at the parish prison in New Orleans, so I already had it down to a science. I could work that thing with one hand. One day I was there and "Every Day" came on the radio. I felt like, "Oh wow, that's me!" At the end, the DJ said, "That was Mr. Aaron Neville."

Sarge said, "You mean Mr. 016955," and we both had a laugh.

11

Tell It Like It Is

I came back to New Orleans at the end of 1964 and met my new daughter, Ernestine. We'd started her when I was home before my sentencing, and she was born while I was at Wayside Rancho. I had two more years of probation to serve in California, but they let me do it back home in New Orleans. We moved into a house on Chestnut Street, and Joel's aunt gave us a car.

I was strong and clean and healthy—probably the healthiest I had ever been. And I thought I was finished with my crazy life. But I wasn't. Me and Melvin hooked back up and pretty soon I started dabbling in heroin again.

Don't get me wrong, I wasn't out in the streets all the time. I took care of Joel and our three children. I never took any money away from my family for my habit. But when I worked a few days on the riverfront, which paid really well, I would put a little on the side for the dope. I used to do up and hang by my friend Snooks's house and nod. I mostly got high on the weekends.

Sometimes I stayed away from it for a good long while, but then an old friend would pass by outside and give a little whistle that meant he'd scored or was going to. And that whistle did something to me inside. I just had to go.

I had my fair share of jobs, and I was never afraid of hard work. I worked on the docks. I drove trucks. I worked for Boh Brothers Construction digging in the dirt and mud to bury cables underground. I worked building prefabricated houses. I worked at an ironworks where nothing in there weighed less than a hundred pounds. I worked with a friend of mine, Earl Preston, pouring concrete to make driveways. Me and another friend, Vernon Bellings, painted houses. I really liked that job, because you had a lot of freedom and I always wanted to do the best paint job I could, be proud of our work, and make the boss proud of our work. He would trust me and Vernon to go and start jobs ourselves.

I believe the best job I had back then was working on the docks as a longshoreman, loading and unloading cargo ships. If you worked three days, you had a really nice payday—way more than you would have had on a regular job. And if you worked the graveyard shift overnight, you got time and a half or sometimes double time.

I would go to the hiring hall at six a.m. and stand among many guys trying to get work, and the foremen would always hire me because they knew I came to work. There were guys coming out and getting hired, but when they got to their designated jobs they'd start doing a rain dance—"Bro, I sure wish it would rain so I could go home."

I'd say, "Why the hell you come out here faking like you want to work? Somebody else who really wanted to work could've had that job."

The good thing about the work was you were never in the same spot. If you got hired, they would send you to one of the many wharves from New Orleans on up to Luling and Hahnville, Louisiana. You started the work at eight a.m., so you needed a car, or you got a ride from someone going to the same location.

It was exciting work—plenty hard, but you didn't have anyone over you telling you what to do. You knew what you were supposed to do, so you just went and did it. We unloaded stuff like sacks of coffee, cotton bales, oil drums, bales of rubber. Sometimes I worked a grain boat. I believe that's how I first messed up my lower back, lifting that heavy shit. I didn't know about using my legs to lift with; we were young dudes and would just bend and lift, manhandling the stuff with sheer strength, but really it was manhandling us. The old guys used to stand around and watch the young bucks like me killing ourselves. They'd already figured out the better way to lift that stuff, using their legs, and they'd make it look easy. But they left us to figure it out for ourselves.

I liked and appreciated the job while I had it because it served a greater purpose, which was supporting my family. A lot of guys in Louisiana took care of their families and sent their kids to school working as longshoremen. Years later you started to see the jobs dwindle, though. They started having palletized goods in containers; that put so many humans out of jobs and the riverfront work started getting small.

I remember I used to sing down in the hole of the ship because it had cool acoustics—that natural reverb. The guys would tell me, "Bro, you shouldn't be down in this hole. You should be on the radio and TV like Smokey Robinson and the Isley Brothers."

I would say, "Bro, I have a family to feed so I have to be down in this hole. My time will come to get up out of this hole."

Sometimes I worked for a place called Superior Wholesale, owned by Tony and Nick—two Italian guys who used to work for the Quaglino Tobacco and Candy Company on Claiborne Avenue. Eventually they stole enough stuff from there to open their own store, so they started Superior Wholesale. They had customers all up and down southern Louisiana, and they hired me, Marvin, his brother Johnny, and our friend Stackolee as drivers. They paid us fifty dollars a week, so we had to take cartons of cigarettes from the storehouse to make it make sense, moneywise. Each time we went out of the storehouse we were strapped with cartons of cigarettes, which we would sell on the street. In the evening at knock-off time, we'd be back in the store and Tony would be sitting at his desk and tell me to reach up to the top shelf for a box of candy. He was really patting me down, because when I reached up my shirt would go high up so he could see if I had anything under it. But it was too late then, because the goods were already gone. After selling the cigarettes, I had money for my family, plus score money.

Hurricane Betsy slammed New Orleans in September 1965. We didn't have a car at the time, so we couldn't leave. We rode it out at home. Ivan was six then, Aaron was three, and Ernestine was two. I thought we'd be okay, but it was scary as shit. The walls seemed to be breathing; they were moving in and out and making moaning sounds. I was standing in the middle of the living room with my arms out, trying to hold them up myself. There was an old lady who lived upstairs, and the wind was stronger up there, so she wanted to come down with us. But every time she tried, the wind just blew her back up. I never knew it could blow like that inside a house. It went on all day, and seemed like even longer.

Some people said the mayor ordered the levees by the industrial canal to be dynamited so the downtown area wouldn't be flooded. When the levees broke, it killed some poor people in the lower Ninth Ward—saving the downtown at their expense—and I guess that was a hint of what was on the way for New Orleans with Hurricane Katrina.

Our house wasn't damaged, but a few months later my Great Aunt Lealah let us stay next door to her in a bigger house that she owned on Valence Street. We stayed there until 1991; when she passed, she willed the house to me and my brother Artie.

It was a happy time, being home with Joel and the kids. They all went to St. Stephen Catholic School, so I would either walk the kids to school or drive them. Joel was working at a charity hospital then as a nurse's aide, so I would dress the kids, comb their hair, and put a kind of twist on each side of Ernestine's hair with a ribbon. Joel would call me at home and give me instructions on how to cook rice and beans—that's still the only thing I know how to cook.

Ivan turned out to have the highest IQ in his school, and had a photographic memory too. You only had to show him something once and he never forgot it. As early as five years old, if he heard something it stuck in his mind. I remember Flip Wilson had a skit about Columbus going to find Ray Charles, and Ivan knew it word for word. When we had company over he would put on his show for them, repeating stuff like that. He was a smart little kid.

On the weekends we would go crabbing, to the drive-in movie, to the games or plays the kids were involved in through school, or to Lincoln Beach. Joel would come with me to my gigs at night while some neighbors watched our kids. And we had a nightly ritual on weekdays: Joel would tell people don't call or come around at seven, and we would watch Art Fleming on *Jeopardy* and then *Wheel of Fortune* and see how many questions we could get right.

After Hurricane Betsy blew the roofs off a lot of houses, me and Melvin had plenty of roofing jobs. But when those jobs got scarce, we turned to other things.

That's when George and Sidney, some old friends, came up with a big bunch of good weed and wanted to use my house to manicure it and bag it up. Joel was at work at the charity hospital and the kids were at school, so I said yes. As payment they gave me and Melvin a whole bag of top-notch stuff, plus all the stems they didn't want to mess with; we got another big bag of weed from those stems. I went way uptown on the corner of Cherokee and Ann Streets, where Joel was from, and sold them as dollar joints. They were going like hotcakes, until some guy dropped a handkerchief on the ground to let the narcs know that a drug dealer they were looking for, Tangle Eye Red, was on the corner. It turns out Tangle Eye Red had just got into a car and drove off, but I was standing there with thirty joints, and my skin was kind of red. The cops jumped down on me and I couldn't swallow all those joints, so they arrested me for possession of weed.

When I got busted for that, I was still on probation in California. I thought for sure I was on my way to the penitentiary in Angola—where my brother Charles was doing five years hard labor for two skinny marijuana joints. And I mean hard labor, cutting sugar cane, which was later deemed inhumane. I got caught with thirty joints. I thought I was looking at at least ten years. It felt pretty bleak.

My daddy got me a good lawyer—Clement Perschall, who was known in the courthouse as the man with the big hat because he always wore this wide-brimmed hat in the courtroom. He was a well-respected man, all business, and well known in the court.

And Mr. Perschall was not the only one working for me. Me and Joel and my mother asked St. Ann and St. Jude to pray for me. We went up the stairs on our knees at St. Ann's, and we attended the St. Jude novenas at Our Lady of Guadalupe. God and St. Jude wouldn't let me get sent to Angola. Somehow, Mr. Perschall filed a motion to suppress the evidence and I just walked away from that charge. I'm still not sure how that happened. I do believe that God knew my heart and that I wasn't a bad guy. I was just doing some stupid shit—again.

The next year, 1966, my friends George Davis and Lee Diamond, two New Orleans musicians, asked me to record a song they wrote, "Tell It Like It Is." My contract with Minit Records had finally expired, and I was free to take it on. But I was looking for something more up-tempo and I thought it was just a mediocre song, so I was reluctant. My brother Artie is the one who talked me into it. He said, "No, 'Tell It Like It Is' is the one." And sure 'nuff, it was. We recorded that song and three more for Par Lo records, a New Orleans label where George was the A&R guy. A few months later we added seven more tracks, including one I wrote, "Jailhouse." It ended up as an album that was also called *Tell It Like It Is*.

Being in the recording studio was the bomb. The studio was like a laboratory for me where I was creating great music. I thought it was like being in the kitchen making great food, or painting on a canvas. I couldn't stand to hear recordings of my speaking voice, but I loved my singing voice, so I thank God for it. I had a lot of fun, and I was really hoping this would be the thing that finally got me heard.

I remember my friend Barry Treudeaux, who lived on our block on Valence Street, he would tell me, "Hey, Red, you a bad mofo, bro, and don't let no one tell you different. Your time is gonna come," and I hung on to that.

And it did. "Tell It Like It Is" came out in November 1966, sold about fifty thousand copies just in New Orleans, and went up the charts like wildfire. The single hit number one in the US on the R&B charts and number two in the *Billboard* Hot 100. ("I'm a Believer" by the Monkees was number one.) When I started hearing that song on the radio, it thrilled my soul. They would play it every hour, seems like, and each time it would make my heart jump. I was straight off the streets and suddenly I had a hit record.

12

Payday for the Record Company

When "Tell It Like It Is" hit big, all kinds of people were coming at me wanting to manage me. But most of them had nothing to offer. Par Lo wanted to send me on the road with basically nothing. I asked them what I was supposed to do about clothes, music, photos, a band, and all that, and there were not many answers. One guy told me not to worry about music because most of the places I'd play would have my record on the jukebox to rehearse to. I just laughed at him. They were trying to make it look like they knew what they were doing, but they didn't.

Joe Jones, who was the longtime manager of the Dixie Cups (they recorded "Going to the Chapel") and a New Orleans singer and session guitarist named Alvin Robinson (a.k.a. Shine) stepped in and kind of saved the day. Joe started managing me, and he got Par Lo to give me ten thousand dollars as an advance against the record sales. I was able to buy a car for my dad, who was a cab driver at the time. Joe got me on a tour with a bunch of other groups and got charts written for all my music, and Shine was going to play guitar and be the road manager.

When I was out on the road with Larry, I used to wear his suits, but Joe got me measured up for three suits of my own. It was the first time I'd ever had a custom suit like that. I put one on and looked in the mirror and went, "Whoa, it's me!" It felt amazing seeing myself finally looking like the man I'd always wanted to be. We had professional pictures taken, and I still keep one in my office. You can practically see the sun shining out of my face. I was twenty-five and looking sharp.

For two months I toured in the Carolinas, Florida, Ohio, and everywhere in between as part of a big show, and it was always sold out. I was sharing the stage with the great Otis Redding, the Marvelettes, the Drifters, the Shirelles, and James and Bobby Purify (they had a big hit called "I'm Your Puppet"). It was one of the best packages I'd ever been on and a pleasure going on that tour. I was happening.

In those gigs we performed with local musicians as our band, six shows a day. Joe knew all the good guys, and Shine would set it up before we even got there. Shine also knew where to score, so we would go and cop heroin between shows.

I was scheduled to join a big show at the Apollo up in Harlem on Christmas 1966, but a huge blizzard shut down the whole East

Coast. So we took a crop duster plane from Columbus to Lorraine, Ohio, then we rented a Mustang and Shine drove in that blizzard all the way to New York City, because he knew the route. We got there just in time, and our show was held over an extra week at the Apollo. Billy Stewart, Charlie and Inez Foxx, the Falcons, and the Flamingos—who I loved when I was a kid—were on that show.

The first and only time I had chitlins was at that gig at the Apollo Theater. We usually hung out at the theater between shows, and there was a woman who came around selling box dinners. She had one initialed CH for chicken and one labeled CH for chitlins. I asked for chicken and she gave me chitlins. I had no idea what it was. I ate a little of it and said, "Wow, this is some funny-looking chicken," and Barbara Hawkins of the Dixie Cups told me, "That's not chicken, that's chitlins!" I spit it out.

I went out on tour with Otis Redding in the early part of 1967, up and down the Eastern Seaboard, from Canada to Florida, Georgia, the Carolinas, New York. I was on a couple of shows with Little Stevie Wonder, who was about sixteen then, and I remember him walking around by himself backstage—he didn't want anyone to help him. I liked to watch him perform from the side of the stage. He was this little guy blowing his harmonica and walking all around the stage so sure of himself that you'd think he could see. He had a song called "Fingertips" that had first charted when he was just thirteen, and I loved to hear him do it.

Things were a lot more upscale with Otis than when I'd toured with Larry Williams. The Marvelettes had a lady who traveled with them to keep the guys away—they were really cool. We rode in

Greyhound buses and stayed in nice hotels. A lot of the hotels were still segregated, but we tried to go to Hiltons, which were not. Hilton was one of the first hotel chains to desegregate. We stayed in the Hilton in Atlanta. It was the first one with the blue dome and had elevators on the outside, and at that time it was the tallest building in Atlanta. You could see it when you came into the airport.

My dad got to go out with us for about a week, and he and Otis really hung out. Otis was like a country boy, always smiling and nice to everybody. I really liked to watch his act, the way he held the microphone with both hands and walked up and down, so smooth. I loved to hear the way he sang "Try a Little Tenderness"; that was one of his chestnuts.

When I wasn't onstage, I'd spend most of my time at the hotel. I had the dope coming to me, and it was like I was in a cocoon. It was a lonely cocoon. Joel would visit us on the road sometimes, too, but mostly she stayed home to take care of our kids. We were calling each other every day, sometimes more than once. Every time I thought about her, I called. That was in the days before cell phones, so I'd be on the phone at the hotel all the time. When I talked to her, it was like a bright light in my head. It's hard to explain, but being away wasn't so hard when I could talk to her.

Joe was managing Shine, and he ended up with some big hits, including "Something You Got." So early in 1967, right after the tour with Otis, Shine went on the road and Joe sent for my brother Artie to join me. I started touring as a solo act. It was just me, Aaron Neville, with a backup band and my brother Artie directing. Joe was a professional, but he was looking out for his own interests, not mine. When we were touring, Frank Sinatra contacted him and said he wanted to do something with me around "Tell It Like It Is," but Joe didn't let me know about it and messed it up. I didn't find out about it until it was too late—Barbara Hawkins of the Dixie Cups told me what happened.

Me and Artie were touring up and down the East Coast. We covered some New Orleans standards and all my hits, plus the R&B songs that were hot then. Everybody loved it. We were up in Montreal when we got the news that our father had had a fatal heart attack. We went home right away. They brought Charles home in shackles from Angola Penitentiary for the funeral.

My dad, Arthur Sr., was only fifty years old—too young. He was a hard-working man all his life. When he stopped sailing, he had jobs like furniture mover and taxi driver, and he was also a counselor at the Milne Boys Home, where Louis Armstrong had learned to play his horn. Some of the boys from the home came to his funeral, and you would've thought he was their father, they cried so hard.

After we buried Poppee, me and Artie went back on the road playing and singing. I thought "Tell It Like It Is" was going to be my big break—which it wasn't. I don't think God was ready for me to have that kind of success. I still had some growing up to do. Plus I wasn't ready to leave the drugs alone, and Artie got tired of my shit and decided to go back to New Orleans. Shine came back and acted as my road manager and band director for a while, and then I was on my own. Joe set me up with gigs, and I'd be at a club for a couple of weeks sometimes, hanging out there by myself. It could get pretty lonely.

I spent a month playing at a club in Tampa, Florida, with a blues singer named Latimore. I would do six or seven songs, Latimore did about the same, and the band did some. They were rocking shows, and even when I was jonesing, the music and the crowds made me feel good and not think about the bogeys.

One night Jimi Hendrix and the two fellows who played with him came into the club and wanted to sit in with us. This was after he'd played the Monterey Pop Festival and he was crazy famous. I knew who he was and he knew who I was; that's why he came to the club. I remember him wanting to play on the song I was singing, "Knock on Wood." He took a badass solo, and another one on "Tell It Like It Is" that was awesome. He played with me for my whole set, and I was grinning like the Cheshire Cat, ear to ear. That was one hell of a night. I had big respect for Jimi, and I know he's in the heavenly band now taking mean solos.

In Tampa I stayed at a hotel that was owned by some Black ladies who were retired old-time vaudeville players. It was a nice place with a swimming pool, and I'd sit out there with a soldier and his wife and smoke weed.

By then Charles had gotten out of Angola, after serving three and a half years, and he moved to New York and hung out there with a singer from New Orleans he knew named Willie. I would send money to them in New York and they'd send me drugs in Florida right in the US mail. One day I got the package and, knowing that I had more coming soon, I shot it all up. But the next package didn't come. They'd bought the heroin with my money and shot it up themselves and didn't send me any. But I didn't know that. I freaked out thinking the police had found the dope and I was gonna be busted.

I was so paranoid that I had the hotel change my room. But that didn't solve the bigger problem. I was getting bogey, jones was coming down, and that night I was tossing and turning so much that I flipped the whole mattress off the bed. The next morning when I woke up, a little old guy who cleaned the rooms came and saw me. He was kind of bent over and looked like he had been through it— and I guess that's how he figured out right away what I was going through.

He said, "Hey, youngblood, looks like you're in a bad way."

I said, "Yeah, bro, it's rough."

So he said, "I got these few morphine tablets I can let you have to get the bogeys off of you."

I said, "Wow, man. God must've sent you."

I asked him, did he know where I could cop some more?

He said, "Bro, you sit out by the pool with him just about every morning."

The next morning I asked that soldier, "Why didn't you tell me you were holding?"

He said, "You never asked."

I said, "Well, I'm asking now." So I was set then and didn't have to send to New York for my stuff.

Another stop I remember from that tour was one of the prettiest places in the country—Aiken, South Carolina. It's right near Augusta, Georgia, where James Brown bought the radio station he used to shine shoes in front of. I wanted to be the kind of famous where I could do things like that. Anyhow, I was there for a couple of weeks playing a club, and I had my usual arrangement with Charles, but it was another time when the drugs from New York didn't come. I was on my own and withdrawing off of heroin. I decided to just try and roll with it.

Some people who lived in Aiken had come to my show and then come backstage to talk with me. Somehow we just really hit it off, and I put them on the guest list for the remainder of my shows. They invited me to come and stay with them at their place. They had no idea what I was going through and that they were helping me to get through it. I told them I was fighting the flu.

They had about a hundred acres. It was autumn, and the trees were so beautiful—every color you could think of. Being from New Orleans, I'd never seen a fall like that before. They took me hunting with them. I didn't want to shoot anything, so I would just shoot the gun in the air, but I liked being out there in the woods with them. I remember one of their kids was this young guy whose arm had been torn off in some kind of machine accident, but he mastered that other arm. Nothing got past him; a rabbit had no chance with him and his gun.

I stayed with them for a week or so, and their kindness and hospitality is one of my fondest memories. I was on the other side of my sickness quickly. I can't remember their names anymore, but I thank those people. They're in my sweet reverie.

I was supposed to hook up with Otis Redding and his band on that trip, but the business end just didn't work out. I was bummed, but I guess St. Jude was looking out for me again. Otis's career was skyrocketing then, and he and his band had chartered a private jet. On December 10, 1967, they were flying from Cleveland to Madison, Wisconsin, for a concert. The weather was bad and the plane crashed into a lake. Otis and the other six guys on board all died. We got to be real tight when we were touring together, so if I'd been on that tour with him, I probably would have been on that plane. Otis was only twenty-six, and he had recorded "Sittin' on the Dock of the Bay" just a few days before. He never got to sing it live.

"Tell It Like It Is" was at the top of the R&B charts for a long time, and even reached number two on the pop charts at a time when the whole world was going crazy for the Beatles. It charted in Canada, too. Everybody wanted to buy that record. But Par Lo was too small, and they couldn't keep up with the demand. The distributor they worked with, Dover, went bankrupt in 1968, and so did Par Lo. In the end, all I got was that ten-thousand-dollar advance.

It was a payday for the record company, but not for me. When I look back at it now, though, I say God knew what He was doing. He probably figured that if I had got all that money back then, I wouldn't be here now.

13

A Crack in My Heart

When Artie got sick of me being deep in the dope and left my tour in 1968, he started his band back up in New Orleans. Art Neville and the Neville Sounds was Artie plus George Porter on bass, Zigaboo Modeliste on drums, Leo Nocentelli on guitar, and Gary Brown on sax. I came home from touring and joined them. We played this uptown place called the Nite Cap, which for a while was *the* place to play, and we would pack it every night.

That's really when I got hip to just how badass Cyril was. I knew he could sing, but he was going over and above. He would do James Brown better than James Brown, and meanwhile Gary was playing the shit outta his sax. Cyril used to do this song called "Jealous Kind of Fellow"—he just confiscated the song as his own.

Then Artie and his rhythm section got a chance to play a club in the French Quarter called the Ivanhoe, and that's where the Meters were born. They became the house band for Allen Toussaint and his record label, Sansu Records. The Meters were a badass funky band, and they called Artie Poppa Funk.

Me and Cyril hooked up with Sam Henry, who was an incredible Hammond B3 organ player, to form Sam and the Soul Machine. Gary Brown joined us on sax, and Richard Amos or sometimes Paul Boudreaux was on bass, Eugene Sinegal on guitar, and Robert Bull Dog Bonney on drums. We were a force to be reckoned with. We played the Nite Cap, Prout's Club Alhambra, the Greystone Lounge, and all the big clubs. Sam and the Soul Machine ended up being the premier band in New Orleans in the late 1960s and early '70s. It was a dynamic band—and I mean that literally. Cyril used to do splits, and Gary would do actual flips while he was playing the saxophone.

The Nite Cap was a Black club; the Ivanhoe was white. (The Ivanhoe was directly across the street from the Driftwood Lounge, where I played with the all-blind band when I was fifteen years old. There were still no Black clubs in the French Quarter.)

Sam and the Soul Machine would play at least five nights a week, sometimes from ten p.m. to three or four in the morning. Around Mardi Gras time we would play till daybreak. We would have those people—doctors, lawyers, the cream of New Orleans—packed wall to wall, screaming and hollering and sweating and dancing. They were snorting coke in the bathroom and having a very wild, very good time. Sometimes at the Nite Cap, some of the football players from the New Orleans Saints would be there grooving until we quit.

We were all doing a lot of drugs back then, so in the Soul Machine we took breaks for over an hour and a half looking to score and the audience would just wait for us. Sometimes the club owner at the Greystone paid me with heroin, which made things easier.

One night when we were playing at a big fancy club called the Desert Sand on Claiborne and Esplanade in the Sixth Ward, some guy slapped Cyril's girlfriend. Cyril ran outside to confront him, and I tried to get out there to help him. But the club was so crowded that by the time I pushed my way outside, Cyril had the dude pinned against a brick wall. I saw something shiny in the guy's hand. I was trying to get to Cyril but it felt like I was moving in slow motion. When I finally got there, I looked at his neck and saw his jugular vein exposed. The rest of the band came out and we all kicked the guy's ass. Then we drove Cyril to the hospital, where he got a bunch of stitches in his neck, then came back and finished the gig.

In March 1970 my sister Cookie lost the last of her battles with her health. She was just eighteen. We buried her in her prom gown and a tiara. She looked like Sleeping Beauty—so beautiful that people were taking pictures of her in her coffin. We were all devastated. Cookie was so young, and we couldn't understand how she had to leave that soon.

The next year, when I was thirty, my son Jason was born and our family was now six people. Then in 1972 I cut a single called "Baby I'm a Want You" for Sansu that came out on Mercury Records. I thought it was a great song, but it didn't really go anywhere for me. The year after that I recorded "Hercules," also for Sansu on Mercury Records, but there were problems with the pressing and it never really got a proper release. I was making enough money to support my family, but it still meant a lot of hustling and plain hard labor to make it happen. I was working on the docks all day, gigging all night, and watching the promise of "Tell It Like It Is" slip away. I wanted to be a singer—not a part-time singer but a man who makes his living by singing.

All the day-to-day shit of living in New Orleans was getting to me, too. Me and my friends were getting picked up by the police as a regular thing—a lot of times for nothing at all that we could see. One time me and my buddy Jake (the one I wrote the song "Brother Jake" about) were hanging around this club called the Robin Hood looking to score, and the police swooped down on us and grabbed us up. One of them stood on the corner with us while the other one walked down the sidewalk. We could see right where he was heading: There was a white handkerchief in the bushes. We knew what it was right away, and so did the cops. Guys used to stash their works till they scored their dope, because if the police found a rig and cooker, they would try to find even a tiny grain of heroin in it, and then they could charge you with possession. When the cop pulled the works out of the bushes, Jake yelled, "I don't know who that rig belongs to, but I can take you to my house. I know my works is clean."

They took us to jail and charged us with possession—even though they hadn't actually found any heroin. That was part of the norm down there. The police would grab on to anything they could to lock somebody up and see if they could get a case on them.

We were locked up in the parish prison for a couple of months, until they finally had to let us go because there was no evidence of heroin—or that those works were even ours. One evening we were in the prison dayroom when this guy just passed out. We knocked down for him on the iron columns in the dayroom to call the guards, and they came up and took him out on a stretcher. As they were leaving with him, one of them said, "We don't know what to do for him. We don't know if it's heroin or methadone."

A couple of nights later, Jake said, "Hey, y'all knock down for me," and we did. He lay down on the floor with his tongue hanging out. The guards came up and put him on a stretcher and were headed out when one of them said, "We don't know what to do for him. We don't know if it's heroin or methadone." And Jake, still with his tongue hanging out, whispered, "Methadone." They threw him off the stretcher and said, "Get your ass back on that tier!"

That gave us something to laugh about for weeks. Three o'clock in the morning you would hear somebody yell out, "Methadone," and the whole tier would be cracking up. It kind of broke up the stale air.

I still laugh when I think about that, but it wasn't funny getting arrested for being in the vicinity of someone else's works, and then being away from your family and out of work for months.

If I went to jail there was nothing Joel could do but try to get me out. Most of the time she'd call her Aunt Tanteen, who owned a nice bar where people who worked in the courthouse sometimes hung out. She was well connected and well respected, and she could sometimes get my case dismissed or at least help get me out sooner.

To raise money to bail me out or to pay for a lawyer, Mommee and her sisters would sometimes give a supper at our house and people from the neighborhood would pay for the food. It wasn't uncommon at the time—people would give a supper to pay for their rent and things like that. My Auntie Lena and Auntie Odile were real good cooks, so their suppers always did well. One time they made stewed chicken that was so good that it sold out fast. A guy came for the chicken and my aunt said, "We're out of chicken, we just got the gravy."

He said, "Then give me the gravy and some rice."

Joel was always in my corner when I got arrested. She was mad at the police, not me. The police just seemed to be happy to arrest you, never mind whether you did something or not. And that could get damn dangerous. One day I was standing at a bus stop when this police car pulled up to the red light and the cops went to staring at me and looking at some kind of photo. Then they backed up, stopped by me, and got out and came up to me. One of them said, "You're not under arrest, but the detectives want to have a word with you."

I asked, "What is it about?"

They said, "Oh, we don't know. All we know is that it's a dangerous charge."

I knew I hadn't done anything like that, so I got in the car and went to the detective bureau.

And that's where I found out that they'd picked me up because they said I "fit the description to a T" of a guy who'd raped and murdered a seventeen-year-old white girl and threw her body into a dumpster on St. Claude Street behind a Church's Fried Chicken. Really? I fit the description to a T? Did that guy have a big mole over his eye and a tattoo of a dagger on his cheek? I said, "I hope y'all catch his ass, looking that much like me and doing crazy shit like that."

The detective asked me if I had an alibi for the night that girl was murdered. It happened on Christmas Eve, and I was singing with the Soul Machine at the Nite Cap that night, so I said, "I have about four hundred alibis." They had to let me go, but just thinking about it gives me a chill. If I hadn't had an alibi, that would've been my charge—and probably the end of my life, because back then they had the electric chair in Louisiana. Something big like that the police just wanted to solve; they didn't really care if they got it right. I thank God for being with me at that moment, but I do think about how many innocent people were locked up, or worse, for something they didn't do.

The pain and frustration I was feeling about how everything was going down then is what led me to keep sticking a needle in my arm. Most of my friends, they didn't have something big to reach for. Maybe somebody took it away from them, like the nuns at school who told Charles he couldn't be a scientist. Maybe they didn't have anything in the first place. And without that big *something*, their lives were just ticking away.

Yes, I wanted to be famous, but it was a lot more than that. Singing purified me. When I was onstage, I was closest to my true self, closest to God. My heart was turned inside out so everyone could hear what was in it. When I wasn't singing, I was an angry, drugged-out thug with a voice like an angel but no reason to be one.

I was also hanging out with a lot of shady characters. One of my running buddies was a guy named Treacherous Slim, a tall, dark-skinned guy who I grew up with. I knew him as a nice guy, but

somewhere along the way he'd gone full-on stupid. I was not someone to be messed with, but Slim was a whole other story. He got that
name because he stabbed a man in a barroom—and not in a fair
fight.

At the time, I cut my singles at Sea-Saint Studios, which was
started by Allen Toussaint and Marshall Sehorn, who had also
founded the label Sansu Records. I'd been cheated before on the
records I made, and I knew it was happening again. In those days,
all kinds of shady shit was happening in the record business. Like
you'd cut a single for one label and they'd sell it to another one and
not tell you, and you wouldn't see a dime. Mostly you'd get some
money when you cut the records, but it was just a few hundred dollars. The label helped themselves to all the rest, no matter how
many records you sold.

I needed some money, so I decided to give Marshall a call. But
whenever I called, this lady would answer the phone and say, "Oh,
Aaron, you just missed him." They were giving me the runaround,
no doubt.

So one day Slim suggested we drive over to Sea-Saint Studios
and get my money. On the way over there he showed me his pistol,
and I told him, "Bro, just be cool." And then we made a plan. I went
to the corner grocery store near the studio, used their phone, and
asked for Marshall. I got the same song: "Oh, Aaron, you just
missed him."

Slim had been watching the studio door, and I asked, "Anybody
come out of there?" He said no. Slim was standing there biting his
bottom lip like he was ready to do something crazy. I told him,

"Slim, I just wanna scare him. I don't wanna do nothing to him. Just be cool, man."

So we went up to the front door of Sea-Saint, I put my hand on the doorknob, and right at that moment Marshall had his hand on the inside doorknob. When he opened it and saw me and Slim standing there, him and the lady I'd talked to on the phone turned chalk-white. She started to say something, and I said, "Shut your lying ass." She shut up.

And then Marshall said, "Oh, hey, Aaron, I was just gonna call you. Come on in." I went in and he gave me five hundred dollars. But I never got a cent more. Which was probably because I didn't bring Slim around there again.

This guy named Anthony, who had a connection with a pharmacist, turned me and Slim on to some pills called Dilaudid. It was a strong opiate, so it made your jones really strong—the withdrawal was killer. I remember Anthony had been coming around every day bringing us the dope, then one day he didn't show up. Slim's wife had a car, so we took it and rode down Anthony. Slim pulled a gun on him and said, "Look, sucker, you came uptown and turned us on to that Dilaudid and got us strung out. Now you better be uptown every day or I'll come to your momma's house and get your ass." So do I have to say that Anthony came around every day after that?

Here's how crazy the dope game got. I remember once me and Cyril scored some good dope. We were by my boy Snooks's house with Lil Bobby Smith, Poochie Boo, and Stackolee (who was married to my sister Athelgra). We were doing up, and Cyril went down. I mean he wasn't breathing, wasn't reacting for a long time. They were giving him mouth-to-mouth, beating on his chest, no response. Finally they said, "Bro, ain't nothing more we can do."

I said, "Man, don't stop." All I could think about was what would I tell Mommee if Cyril died. So they brought him outside into the cold air and dragged him back and forth for quite a time.

All of a sudden, he started coming around. He was talking all slow and funny, and the first thing that came out of his mouth was, "Damn, that was some good shit! I want some more."

I said, "Bro, we all will kick your ass talking that shit." We all laughed, but it wasn't funny. Everyone had lost their high worrying about how Cyril could've died.

I was a lost soul then. That's the truth of it. I think Joel knew I was back on the horse but wouldn't let on. Maybe she was kidding herself, maybe she just loved me too much to say anything. We never talked about it. I kept telling myself that it was okay because I was never high while I was home with our kids, because I wasn't shooting up every day, because I didn't take money from them to buy my dope. I learned how to maneuver it and keep these things separate. But even though I was at someone else's house when I was nodding, I would still come home high. And I was home a lot less because I was spending my time at the shooting gallery. I tried to maintain because I had to work. But when I wasn't shooting up, I was smoking weed and I had to take a pill—what I called a stumbler—to get to sleep.

When I got busted for weed in 1965, Joel and I didn't fight about it, and I promised not to do heroin anymore. That's when I started using makeup to cover up my tracks. I couldn't face my family if they knew I was shooting up. It wasn't shame, but something else. I was living a double life.

One night early in 1973, I came home and our house was empty. Joel had had enough, and packed up the kids and moved in with her parents in Pontchartrain Park. She'd decided to try and let me shake the stupid off on my own.

Maybe she knew how bad things had got and didn't want to confront me. Maybe someone in the neighborhood told her. By the time she left me I was gone too far, so maybe I did come home and nod out—I don't remember.

I felt like I'd been knocked out and stomped on. Joel was everything. She and I got married when I was just a kid, and I never really had grown up. I was lower than low, below zero. She paid the bills, ran the house, and everything else, and I didn't know about any of that. But I also didn't know how to have a life without her. Losing her, that just made a crack in my heart.

Joel's parents had forbidden her to see me, but I used to hang out in the park near her house and my son Ivan would sneak outside to talk to me.

I stayed with my mother for a little while. One night she came home and found me slumped over the toilet with a syringe sticking out of my arm. She took it out and put some ice around my neck to try to bring me out of the nod. When I came around, she took me to pray.

After Mommee moved in with Athelgra and her husband, I sometimes stayed with Treacherous Slim and his wife, Rose. She used to tell me, "Aaron, I feel that Slim is gonna kill me." Eventually he did, and went to Angola for it. Sometimes I just roamed the streets, a homeless man. Trying to maintain without Joel was pure hell.

I remember one of my worst days, I was sitting in the gutter in front of an area I used to call the snake pit—three dive bars on Lyons Street. I was in a bad way, confused, and all of a sudden I thought of "Ave Maria." I had first heard it at St. Monica's Catholic School when the choir would sing it at mass, and I was fascinated with the tune. I never knew what the words meant until later—it was in Latin—but every time I heard it, it did something to my heart and soul. And later on in life, it became a light at the end of the tunnel for whatever I was going through. I would get a cleansing feeling. That sound of praising the Blessed Lady was like a saving grace for me, especially when I was at the bottom of a pit, like I was at that moment.

I started singing it to myself, and somehow I felt better from it. That music and God got me up out of the gutter. But it could not close that deep crack in my heart.

And then me and Cyril decided to go up to New York for a while and hang with Charles. You already know what happened there.

14

Left-Handed Shit

I started calling Joel when I was in New York, because I was fed up with what I was doing there and I missed my family so bad. I told her I was ready to straighten up and come back home to her and the kids. I promised her I was going to be right, that I wasn't going to be doing the things I was doing, messing with drugs. She said she still loved me, but she just wanted me to shake the stupid out.

In 1974 I was back in New Orleans, and we got back together at the end of that year and moved into our old house on Valence Street. Ivan was about fourteen, Aaron was twelve, Ernestine was eleven, and Jason was about three years old.

After that, Joel stuck with me through the rest of her life. She helped me grow up—as much as I ever have. She kept that little boy in me in check. I believe that she also gave me a reason for wanting to live a better, cleaner life.

I finally got to know and hang out with Jason, my youngest. He would get away with a lot of shit because he was the baby. He was smart, inquisitive, and would take all kinds of chances. Like one time he was swinging on the shower curtain and fell in the tub and busted his head. That was one time I stood there and watched the doctor sew up his head, but it wasn't the last. The next time he was climbing up the doorframe and busted his head again. One day he and his friend found a gun and decided to go for a bike ride with it. His friend had the gun while Jason was riding on the handlebars. When the bike hit a bump the gun went off, shooting Jason in his back about an inch from his spine. That took a few years off me and Joel, watching him in the hospital.

Ivan started getting interested in music and asked me to show him something on the piano. I did, and he took it from there. He got some pointers from his Uncle Artie, and from the great New Orleans pianist James Booker, who was a friend of ours, but his mind was working overtime. Plus he was ambidextrous, so he took it to another level. He could do with his left hand what most people couldn't do with their right hand, plus he could sing. He started playing in the talent shows and was winning them.

I was back working on the Mississippi River docks then, loading and unloading boats, and gigging on the weekends. I was just trying to take good care of my family. I laid off the heroin for a little while, but the stupid wasn't finished with me yet.

I tried the Ts and blues for a bit. From the 1960s through the early '80s, my running partner was Tyrone Gayton (a.k.a. Rooney). I had an old Buick that Joel's Aunt Tanteen gave me, and me and

Rooney and my brother Cyril would be running down the heroin. When there was a panic on the heroin, we ran to cough syrup and Ts and blues. They sold them in sets—one pill was pentazocine (an opioid) and the other was tripelennamine (an antihistamine). You crushed them up and then cooked the powder just like heroin. Then you drew it up in the syringe and shot it in your vein.

Ts and blues were an adventure you took. I still wonder who was the first one to try that shit. Anyway, I did them for quite a while off and on. It wasn't habit-forming, just a constant want. I can't describe the feeling—sort of euphoric, a rush. More of an upper than a downer. And I could act more natural on them, so me and Joel was cool.

I still had a yearn for heroin, but sometimes it was scarce, and anyway the sets seemed easier to manage—although I had seen dudes having a seizure when they took it. One time when Rooney wasn't around, me and Cyril went by these guys over in the Twelfth Ward, Big Yipe and Bubbee, to do the Ts and blues. When I came down from the high, Bubbee told me that I'd had a seizure (that's right, I wasn't aware). That was the end of Ts and blues for me. Heroin felt safer.

I did get bunked a few times, though. One time me and Stackolee scored from this dude and he sold us some stuff that gave us chills and fever. I was in the bed shivering for hours. When we came around, we went back around there and kicked his ass.

One morning in 1975, my mother called to wake me up to go look for work at the longshoremen's hall. I went out but nothing was shaking, so I came home. When I got back, my brother Cyril told me that Mommee had been run over by a truck. Mommee, the sweetest lady on the planet, was on her way to work, had the right of way after getting off the bus at Tulane and Galves, and this guy in a moving van was in a hurry, went around the bus, turned the corner, and ran over her, front and back wheels.

I went out looking for him, but God didn't let me find the dude that day. I'm glad He didn't, because my life would have taken a whole different turn, no doubt. But that day I couldn't sit with it, so I did the only thing I knew how to do: I went out and scored and shot up.

Mommee lived maybe a day or two, and when we went to see her at the hospital, she joked with me and Athelgra. "Remember when I told y'all to always have on clean underwear when you go out just in case something like this would happen? Well, forget it, 'cause when that truck ran over me I spoiled myself." Then she told us she was going to be with Poppee.

I once heard a minister say that when his time came to stand in front of the Lord for judgment, all he could think to say would be, "Lord, I tried, and I hope that I have done your will." I feel the same way. I've tried to walk the path He set for me, and even the times I went astray, I could feel His presence. He's carried me through some dangerous terrain. I kept my faith because what I felt whenever I sang, I knew it was something bigger than me. It gave me a peaceful feeling; that's why I called it medicine. I felt rich sometimes just because of the voice that God let me use while here on Earth. Even when I was frustrated and angry and doing the drugs, always in the back of my mind I felt that I was gonna be able to be heard.

I tried to not ever have hate anywhere in my heart. I looked at everyone who crossed my path as my brother or sister, and I tried to always see God in everyone no matter what skin color they had. I always tried to look further and deeper. I used to say I want to see the world through God's eyes and the world to see Him in me. I learned all that from my mother. Mommee was a nurse's aide at the same charity hospital where Joel worked, and the patients she helped just loved her. She was the kindest person I ever met. It shone in her eyes and she embedded it into her children. The day she died was the saddest day of my life.

Just a few months later, I had to call on St. Jude again—this time without Mommee to add her prayers. A so-called friend named Sonny, a singer from New Orleans, came to me looking to score some cocaine. He kept on asking and I kept on telling him no, but I finally gave in and scored for him. It was good coke, and he scored some more. That's when he brought his boy Freddie to me. I trusted Sonny, so I thought nothing of it. I scored for Freddie twice, but I started to have a bad feeling about it. The third time Freddie called and asked me to score, I said, "No, bro, that dude's gone out of town."

So he said, "Well, do you know anywhere to score heroin?"

I said, "No, bro, I ain't no dealer. I was just doing Sonny a favor." I got this feeling that I call mother wit, like a second sense, and I knew it was some left-handed shit. But it was too late.

An hour later about ten people came knocking on my door, and they were all the police. There was Freddie in a gray suit, a Starsky and Hutch gun at his side. It turns out Freddie was an undercover narc. Sonny got busted and made a deal to give someone else up. I got busted as a dealer, and that's a federal offense.

And it got worse. My lawyer told me to pray I didn't get Judge Edward G. Boyle, well known as the hanging judge because he loved to hand out long sentences. But when we got the court papers, there was his name.

Me and Joel started going to St. Ann's shrine and crawled up the steps on our knees, asking St. Jude to pray for me again. We went to the novenas at the shrine of St. Jude at Our Lady of Guadeloupe, and I sang there—the deepest kind of prayer. We prayed overtime, asking God for another miracle.

The truth is I wasn't a dealer, but I was found guilty on both counts. When I went to court for sentencing, I stood in front of the judge and he sentenced me to one to fifteen years in the federal penitentiary. For some reason, though, I wasn't really afraid. After what seemed like a very long time, Judge Boyle added, "I don't know why I'm doing this, but I'm going to suspend that sentence and put you on three years' probation."

I said, "Thank you, Your Honor, and thank you, God and St. Jude." Just like in California, God had softened that judge's heart and saved me from the penitentiary. I guess He had other plans for me.

As me and Joel and a couple of friends who came to court with me were walking out of the courtroom, we passed by the federal marshal, a Black guy with a really mean look. He showed me the chains in his hands and said to me, "I don't know who you had in this courtroom with you, but these shackles was for your ass." He was really pissed off.

I felt a cold chill up my spine, and I made a solemn vow. "If you didn't get me this time, you can forget it. I ain't coming back in nobody's court again." And I never have.

15

The Mighty Neville Brothers

It all started in the early 1970s when Uncle Jolly started masking with the Indians and got to be the big chief. He had a krewe called the Wild Tchoupitoulas. Tchoupitoulas Street in New Orleans is the through street closest to the Mississippi River, and the Chapitoulas were the Native Americans (now long gone) who used to live there. In Choctaw, the name means "those who live by the river." We're all part Choctaw, so it seemed to fit.

The Wild Tchoupitoulas used to deck out in really elaborate regalia and do a cool call-and-response routine during Mardi Gras parades. Uncle Jolly was living next door to me and Joel, and I would go over to watch him and help sew all those beads and sequins and feathers on his Indian suit. Sometimes his fingers would bleed from getting stuck by the needles. The Indians made a new suit every year, and his whole krewe would sew on their suits all year long. It was definitely a ritual, more than just sewing a suit. You feel free when you're out in the Indian suit. It's hard to explain it, but this is the one day where the police don't bother you and nothing else matters. You're just out there with your krewe, everybody looking after everybody else.

Like I said before, the Indian tradition probably comes from slave times, when the Native Americans helped out runaway African Americans. What we call Indian music in New Orleans has West African and Caribbean roots. The Mardi Gras parades may have also come from slave times. Back then, on Sundays slaves would gather in Congo Square (in what's now Louis Armstrong Park), play their music, and sing and dance. After the Civil War, all that ended and New Orleans was segregated. Black people were not allowed in the Mardi Gras parades, and they started forming tribes, masking (putting on the regalia), and holding their own parades. The routes are always secret, even today, and nobody gets a parade permit or anything official like that. The big chiefs decide where they're going, and the krewe goes there.

Uncle Jolly was the big chief, who leads his krewe not just at Mardi Gras but all year. Some tribes have a second chief and a trail chief too, but the big chief is the one in charge. In the parade, though, the chief doesn't walk at the front of the krewe. That's the spyboys, who go out and check the terrain to see if another krewe is coming. Then comes the flag boys, who carry the krewe's flags and use them to relay back any intel from the spyboys.

The big chief is next, in the center of his krewe, directing what they all do. And behind him is the wild man, who carries a hatchet or a knife. Up until about the 1960s, when krewes met they got into fights, and it could be with knives or even guns. But they all decided it was too barbaric, so now when they meet up the fighting is about who has the best regalia and sings and dances best. So the wild man's job these days is to decide who can talk to the big chief.

Uncle Jolly said Mommee had told him she always dreamed of seeing us all perform together. So in 1976, when he decided that he wanted to record some of his traditional New Orleans Indian songs, he got together me, Artie, Charles, Cyril, some members of his tribe, plus the singer Willie Harper, and Artie's band, the Meters, to make a record. It was produced by Allen Toussaint and Marshall Sehorn at Sea-Saint Studio on Clematis Street.

Allen and Marshall started Sea-Saint in 1973, and it lasted until Katrina flooded them out in 2005. They recorded a lot of New Orleans music, and a lot of that ended up on Allen and Marshall's record label, Sansu. The studio got to be pretty famous, and people like Paul Simon, Joe Cocker, Paul McCartney, and Elvis Costello recorded there too.

I was not happy about doing business with Marshall, who had screwed me over big time. But the brothers and my uncle knew nobody else was likely to want to record the traditional New Orleans Indian music, which was big down in NOLA but not so well-known elsewhere, so I went along with it. I was just happy to be going in the studio and doing this music with my Uncle Jolly.

I couldn't wait to start recording with my brothers. When we all went into Sea-Saint to record *The Wild Tchoupitoulas* album, it felt so good. The Indian songs they sing at the parades are call and response, with the big chief as the song leader and the rest of the krewe answering, and a driving, funky beat to keep everyone moving. A lot of the krewes sing the same songs (like "Indian Red" and "Here Dey Come," which were on the album), but the big chief of each tribe puts his own stamp on them, no doubt.

We didn't have any arrangements set or anything like that—it all came together naturally in the studio. And we didn't have to tell anyone what note to take. We just started singing and it came out like we had been singing together for years, when in fact we had never sung all four of us together before then.

We started with "Brother John," a song Cyril and Uncle Jolly wrote about John "Scarface" Williams, big chief of the Apache Hunters krewe, who was stabbed to death in 1972 while he was trying to break up a fight. Cyril wrote "Indians Comin'" on that record too. It was a labor of love doing these songs with Big Chief Jolly and his tribe.

The Wild Tchoupitoulas is a great album, and it's considered a classic of New Orleans party music. Everybody loved it. We toured as the Wild Tchoupitoulas for a while. We wore the Indian regalia too, although not as elaborate as what they wear for Mardi Gras. I wore a beaded vest, headband, and apron. Around Mardi Gras when we played at Tipitina's, we would have people filling up in the neutral ground from Tchoupitoulas to Magazine Street, and we opened the New Orleans Jazz and Heritage Festival that year.

Jazz Fest actually started back in 1970. At the first one, Mahalia Jackson and Duke Ellington joined in a second line in Congo Square. Some heavy-hitting NOLA musicians were there too, including the Meters, Pete Fountain, Fats Domino, and Clifton Chenier. In the beginning not many people came, so you could bring picnic baskets and blankets and have your own spot to lie down on the lawn. By 1975, which was the first time I played there (with a New Orleans band called Bobby Cure and the Summertime Blues, featuring a real great singer named Robyn Casserino), it was held at the Fair Grounds Race Course and had started getting so crazy that there was no space to lie down and you couldn't even bring in your own stuff; you had to buy whatever they were selling.

Going out touring with our Uncle Big Chief Jolly and the Wild Tchoupitoulas Mardi Gras Indians was an exciting adventure. We were taking Mardi Gras to the world, picking up fans along the way. When we played at the Roxy in Los Angeles, Linda Ronstadt and Bette Midler were in the audience—two ladies who helped me later in my career. Ali McGraw was in the audience too, and they all came backstage after to tell us how much they dug our music. (What I remember most about that gig, though, was that there was a lady walking up and down the hallway yelling, "Anybody got blow?")

People were crazy for that album, but it never made much money. Uncle Jolly said it's because we were cheated, and I believe it. Marshall Sehorn had already cheated me and a whole lot of other musicians out of our due (despite that visit from Treacherous Slim). So the Wild Tchoupitoulas never made another album. But we were having such a blast playing together that we decided it was time for all four of us to get together as the Neville Brothers.

We recorded our first album—*The Neville Brothers*—in 1978 for Capitol Records. It had a cool photo on the cover of us walking on the levee, and some great songs. Cyril took the lead on a John Hiatt song called "Washable Ink" and sang the shit out of it. One of my favorites on that album was a Leiber and Stoller song, "Dancing Jones." Artie sang and wrote one called "Speed of Light." Charlie had some great solos. And it's the first time I sang "Arianne," that beautiful Johnny Mathis song.

Jack Nitzsche produced it, and I love that album. It's kind of a mash-up of soul and disco and R&B. But when we played live, there was so much fire and funk that you just don't get in the studio. We were backed at the time by an awesome funk band called Black-male, which was Renard Poché on guitar and his brother Roger on bass, Gerald Tillman on keyboards and great vocals, and Newton Mossop Jr. on drums.

Singing with my brothers, we didn't have to think about it. It was the easiest thing in the world to get our voices together. Artie and me had been harmonizing since the projects, and Cyril already listened and learned. When we got together we knew what we were supposed to be doing without anybody having to say anything. I could look from side to side and see our ancestors in each one of my brothers. I could see my father and my mother in them too—the kindness they taught us, the love and respect they brought us.

When we took the stage, magic happened. If you've ever been to a Neville Brothers show, I know you can still feel it. We held the audience from first note to last. At Tipitina's in New Orleans, we would start playing at midnight and sometimes not end till daylight, and nobody left. It would be packed with people dancing butt to butt, and the place didn't have air conditioning, so it was like being in a sweatbox. I would get home and have to wring my clothes out from sweating so much onstage, and they stank from cigarettes and everything else they were smoking in there. We used to see guys bootie-scooting across the floor in front of the stage. A lot of times we had a real power over the audience. There was this one guy who was hitting his head on an iron post to the beat of the music, and later we learned that he was a lawyer. That was the beginning of the Mighty Neville Brothers.

Our deal with Capitol Records was a one-time thing, and the record didn't really make a lot of money. But we hooked up with promoter and manager Bill Graham that year and started touring. Before that, our managers weren't all that savvy. But Bill kicked down a lot of doors for us, and I have much love and respect for him. He really felt us and wanted to put us in the right direction, almost like he wanted to show us off.

And Bill knew everybody. I always said that if there was a concert on the moon, Bill would've been the promoter. He got us to open for the Rolling Stones, the Grateful Dead, Huey Lewis and the News, Joe Cocker, Boz Scaggs, and a whole lot of others.

Their fans didn't necessarily come to hear a funk band, but they always dug it. When we left the stage, they always wanted more. Carlos Santana once said, "I don't want you to open for us; we'll open and y'all can close." In 1985 when we played the Berlin

Jazz Fest with Dizzy Gillespie, Miles Davis, and Carmen McRae, we were the only non-jazz group in the show and we got three standing ovations. We left fire and smoke behind us wherever we played.

The Neville Brothers played Jazz Fest every year from 1977 to 2012. We usually opened, and that was way cool, but closing on the last Sunday was the special spot. That's the sound the crowd had in their ears and in their blood until the next Jazz Fest. Professor Longhair (a.k.a. Henry Roy Byrd) had that spot until he died in 1980. Then we took over. I'd look out and see a sea of people just totally digging the fire we were bringing. We'd have them out there laughing and crying. And this funny thing I remember is that every year you'd see a couple of birds passing overhead, and they'd always take a crap on the audience. It was hard not to laugh.

From New Orleans, we burned a path across the country. And eventually, we played all over the world—from the Lone Star Café in New York to the Cow Palace in San Francisco to football stadiums in Europe to arenas in Japan. When me and my brothers took to the road, it was a joyous time. God gave us each a hell of a talent, so we were like four fingers that turned into a fist. We knocked 'em dead everywhere we went.

Wherever we performed, people knew all the words to our songs and wanted us to sign their albums. It felt like a poke-your-chest-out time and made us feel all humble. Every gig we played was a special gig. I didn't think about being a star; I just thought about playing some great music.

I was always shy, but I can connect with people onstage—soul touching soul. A lot of times I closed my eyes, and I was there by myself—then nothing intimidated me. I'd become the song, feel the music in my being. Singing, it's like a conversation with God, trying to reach the angels and right the wrongs, sing some notes that will make up for some of the crazy stuff in the world.

Performers can feel what the audience feels, so there's a give and take—we give to them, and they give back to us. A lot of times I would look out into the audience and see people with tears in their eyes, smiles on their faces, hands waving, and I'd know we'd captured their souls. It was always great knowing that what I was feeling, a lot of other people were also feeling it, like the Holy Ghost was in the house. When I sang "Amazing Grace," it felt like we were in church, and then when my brother Cyril took it over with Bob Marley's famous "One Love," he would always remind people that there was only one race, the human race. Some notes can just cut through all the bullshit.

We had a lot of fun out on the road. Sometimes it seemed like our booking agent put a blindfold on and threw darts at a map, because we zigzagged all over the place. But even on the long bus rides, we had a good time just telling stories, reminiscing about our growing up together. We talked about our individual treks through the Calliope and the streets of the Thirteenth Ward, all the trouble we got into and all the shit we got out of.

In the beginning we didn't even think twice about traveling in buses for hundreds of miles, and we shared rooms at hotels.

Sometimes the scenery from the bus window, like the wildflowers along the highway, was really beautiful. Sometimes it was achingly lonely until we reached our destination and got onstage. We weren't making a lot of money, but we were doing what we were born to do. We were boys on the highway, seeking our fortune, so we made the best of it.

I remember me and Brian Stoltz, our guitar player, used to play the game Connect Four while everyone else was trying to sleep in the bunks on the bus. Every time Brian won he would make a sound like Curly from the Three Stooges, and when I won I made a sound like Dr. Ruth, and we would be cracking up. Then all of a sudden from the back of the bus, you'd hear my brother Artie holler out, "Y'all shut up all that damn noise up there!" and that would make me and Brian just crack up laughing.

Bill Graham was famous for saying, "It's not about the money. It's about the money." But while every other promoter I'd worked with meant putting the money in their pocket, Bill meant getting enough so we all could live. And he made good on that.

In 1977 I stopped working as a longshoreman and house painter and every other thing, and worked only as a singer. In 1978 I was able to buy a Ford Thunderbird, the last of the big T-birds. It was a beautiful silver-and-red car—I called it Hi-Yo Silver and Apache Red—and the license plate was APACHE. When me and Joel went to buy it, the salesman was saying, "Hey, you got to see these other cars on another floor."

I said, "I don't need to see anything else. This is the car I want."

The wheels had some way-out rims and the interior was red and silver with some black trim. It was the bomb. I hadn't stolen a car since I did time in the parish prison for it, but I hadn't bought a new one either. That car made me feel like I had finally made it.

My running buddy Rooney liked to keep that car clean. I would come outside in the morning and Rooney would be out there washing it. One morning when I came out, I saw him spit on the rag and wipe something off the car. I told him, "Hey, bro, don't be spitting on the car."

He said, "Bro, the bird just shit on the car," and we had a laugh about it.

Then we'd usually go and score. This was while Joel was at work and the kids were at school, so we would do up where we scored, go around to the barroom, and have a drink and listen to the record player (a.k.a. jukebox) and do our ducking where no one cared, 'cause there would be other cats in there doing the same thing.

On the weekends I took my family for rides. One of our favorite places was Delacroix Island in St. Bernard Parish, about thirty miles from New Orleans, to go crabbing. We would bring a picnic lunch and cold drinks, and we parked right on the side of the water and threw our net in the water with a piece of raw chicken in it, and would pull up a mess of crabs. One time a crab got loose in my trunk, and we didn't know about it for a few days. Man, it smelled the worst! Jason was about seven years old then and was our wild child. We had to tie a rope around his waist and the other end to the car bumper to keep him from jumping in the water.

Being able to take my family out and do these things meant everything. My number-one priority had always been to take care of them, and number two was to be a singer. Now, both were happening. In 1978 I started wearing a St. Jude earring, too—which I still wear today. The patron saint of the impossible had helped make those things possible for me and my family. The path Mommee always had been pointing me to was the path I needed to be on. By the early 1980s, we started making some real money, and by 1989, Joel was able to quit her job and sometimes come out on the road with me.

When we were touring, we'd sing three nights in a row, have one night off, and then three more onstage again. I was always ready to go, as long as I was healthy; a couple of times I wound up in the ER when my asthma got ahold of me. When we weren't on the road, we were working on our next album. So it was 365 days a year.

Looking at it now, I think the Neville Brothers never really got our due because the record companies didn't know how to market us. The studio would put us with some producer who wanted to put his own spin on our music, and we made some off-the-wall recordings that didn't really make sense for us. *Fiyo on the Bayou*, *Yellow Moon*, and the live albums come the closest to who we were onstage.

But on the road, we were a force to be reckoned with—by far the baddest band in the land. My brothers each had something amazing, and a lot of times I would be so mesmerized by their playing and singing that I would forget what I was doing. When Artie or

Cyril was singing and Charlie was blowing, I paid attention. We taught each other.

From the first note to the last, my brothers would have my soul full to the top. Artie (a.k.a. Poppa Funk), my mentor and teacher, would funk you up. When we got onstage he used to say, "We ain't taking no prisoners tonight! School is in session, y'all!" Cyril (the ratty Chin) would give you all the soul you could stand. He was and is as powerful as Bob Marley, James Brown, Marvin Gaye—you name 'em and Cyril is in that number. Charlie (the horn man) could hold his mug among all the other great horn players, including his mentors, like Charlie Parker, Dizzy Gillespie, Miles Davis, and many more. Charles was into the bebop, and he turned me on to a lot of it. He also explained why the jazz musicians started calling each other man, like, "Hey, man. What's up, man. I dig you, man." It was because the white man was calling them boy when they had to go through the back door.

Eric Kolb, who played keyboards and did technical stuff onstage (and died way too young), would announce the band with, "Ladies and gentlemen, I bring you the Mighty, Mighty Neville Brothers." That sounded and felt so great.

Uncle Jolly never got to see our success. I brought him to hospital in 1980, when he had lung cancer, and he said, "I'm not going to see my house again." I got them to put a cot in his hospital room for me. Sometimes I'd leave a gig and go there to sit with him. Joel would sometimes come with me and hold his hands and we'd both pray. Then I'd go in the bathroom down the hall and cry my eyes out until my chest was backward from hurting. He died in August that year.

Over the next thirty-five years we took the stage with just about everybody—Carlos Santana, Peter Gabriel, Sting, Elton John, the Rolling Stones, Tina Turner, Miles Davis, U2—and demanded respect. Anyone whose path we crossed knew our worth, and when we left the stage it was on fire, nothing less. No brag, just fact.

16

Around the World

Me and my brothers from the Calliope Projects, from singing doo-wop on park benches to the Hawketts to the Meters, little did we know that we would become one of the baddest bands in the land.

My brother Artie put the funk to our music. His powerful vocals and badass keyboard playing were a force to be reckoned with. He was the teacher. He guided a lot of the younger musicians—and his brothers. He and Cyril were the original funksters. Cyril I called the soul stirrer; he could sing a song that would put the world on the right track. Charlie was a blowing mofo. He could play with any other horn man and blow them out of the water. He would take you all around the world with his horn, all the places that his life took him, the good the bad and the ugly. I would put the icing on the cake with the high notes, like in "Amazing Grace"; every time I sang that, it was a testimony, coming from deep in my soul. When I had the audience hypnotized with the swirling notes that God made me able to sing, it was a cleansing for me.

The Neville Brothers were on the road for almost forty years. Each one of us got to show our individual talents and our combined talents. We all enjoyed each other's company up and down the road. We never had to tell anyone what to do, what part to take. Everyone knew their note and when to come in on a song. It was like magic—especially watching what we did to the audience. We would have them mesmerized; we brought laughter and tears. The stage was our domain, and we ruled it.

I can't remember how many countries we visited. I do know I've been to every continent except Antarctica. There were some special times, some incredible times, some lonely times, some boring times, some scary times, some magical times. Some moments I will never forget and some moments I can't remember anymore. That's what a life on the road is like.

I'll tell you some of the things I remember, and I'll do my best to put them in order, but I don't remember them that way. We went to so many places so many times that it's hard to remember when some things happened.

Mostly what I remember from the 1980s is a lot of trips to Europe. One year we were there when they said it was the coldest winter in a hundred years. In some places it was twenty or thirty degrees below zero, and when we flew in you could see everything was covered with ice and snow. When we played in Amsterdam all the canals were frozen over. But every city we played, the building was still packed.

We were on this European bus that didn't have the right heating, so we had to sleep in the bunks with all our clothes on under the blankets and we still froze our asses off. The cold really got to Artie, who had a bad back, and eventually he and his son Ian (who had been touring with us) caught a plane and went back home.

In the early 1980s we toured with the Rolling Stones. Ivan was in his early twenties then and came out with us. He got to be really good friends with Keith Richards, and ended up playing in his solo band, the X-Pensive Winos. He also played on the Stones' albums *Dirty Work* and *Voodoo Lounge*. I'm so proud of him.

I've read a lot of stories about how the Stones did a lot of drugs on their tours, but I was clean by then, so if any of that was going on I knew nothing about it. What I mostly remember is that I could hardly understand Mick and Keith when they talked. I'm sure they couldn't understand my New Orleans accent either.

In 1986 and '87 we opened for the Grateful Dead, and they told us not to eat or drink anything anybody handed you. Their fans were into psychedelics and thought it was cool to share. When they played, their fans swarmed all over the place. Two blocks away from the theater it looked like you went into a time warp with all the tie-dyes. After we had played a few shows with them, I ran into this young guy on the street who said, "Hey, man, I saw y'all when you opened for the Dead. I was the one right in front of the stage with the tie-dye."

That made me laugh. I said, "Oh, *you're* the one."

At the New Year's shows with the Grateful Dead, Bill Graham would slide down on this wire as Father Time or the New Year's

Baby, which always got a huge cheer from the crowd. Jerry Garcia really dug us and would call us back onstage to do songs with them. He liked to hang out backstage and jam too. Jerry was a larger-than-life guy. He would always peep over his glasses when he was talking to me, and his smile told me how much he appreciated my voice. We talked about doing some stuff together, but it never panned out. Jerry was definitely a fan of the Brothers, though.

In 1986 we were part of the Amnesty International Conspiracy of Hope tour with Peter Gabriel, U2, Sting, the Police, Miles Davis, Bryan Adams, Lou Reed, Joan Baez, and a bunch of other heavy hitters. That tour was a lot of fun. Musicians are mostly like a family. There's a lot of respect there, and people don't try to push you down so they can get up. So when you travel around with musicians like that, there's just a lot of laughing and clowning around and not a lot of ego. They chartered this big plane for us and as the plane was landing in Iceland the tire blew out. Everybody was scared to death. There was a mountain of talent on that airplane, and I wasn't the only one thinking of Buddy Holly, the Big Bopper, Richie Valens, and the day the music died.

We played in East Berlin in 1987, two years before the Berlin Wall came down. We had to pass Checkpoint Charlie, which was pretty heavy. There were towers all around with armed guards and piles of razor wire. I don't think we even spent the night in East Berlin, so I don't remember much about it except that I was surprised to see they had a McDonald's.

I believe the US government sponsored the show—a free concert with us and Irma Thomas, Barbara Cole, Johnny Adams, and

Solomon Burke—and the people were ecstatic. They were really hungry for that music. I remember when we first got onstage the whole crowd was looking solemn, no smiles on their faces. But when we started playing certain songs, you could see them start to smile then. After everyone had played their sets, me, Irma, and Johnny sang "Amazing Grace," and the people in the audience had their hands in the air and tears in their eyes. It was a really touching experience.

I heard that when they were tearing down the wall in 1989, they played my version of Bob Dylan's song "With God on Our Side." That was special to me. I think I've recorded eight of Bob's songs by now, but that was one of my favorites. Cyril turned me on to Bob Dylan back in 1964 when his album *The Times They Are a-Changin'* came out, because we were ready for the change, being always harassed by the police in those days. Plus we loved the way he looked on that album cover—like he didn't give a shit. Bob was our hero then, and I have much love and mad respect for him now.

In 1988, when we were recording *Yellow Moon* in New Orleans with Daniel Lanois, Bob was there at the same time working with Daniel and stopped by to hear us do "With God on Our Side" and "The Ballad of Hollis Brown." Bob sat in the control room with his jaw resting on his hand, watching me, looking intense. When I finished singing he hugged me; no words needed.

Years later, in 2015, the Grammys honored Bob with the MusiCares Person of the Year Award. He got to pick who he wanted to come to perform his songs, and he reached out to my manager. I said I wanted to sing "With God on Our Side," but Dylan said he thought it was too dark for the show. So he asked me to sing "Shooting Star"—which I had never sung. I read an interview where Bob said, "I could always hear him singing that song for some reason, even when I wrote it." And he said I was "the kind of performer that can do your songs better than you, but you can't do his better than him."

When the Neville Brothers played, it was mostly a funk band, so the soft songs that were in my heart had to be put on the side—songs like "Shooting Star," "Arianne," "Smoke Gets in Your Eyes," "I Only Have Eyes for You," "Stardust," "Ave Maria," and all that beautiful doo-wop from when I was growing up. So around about that time, I got to do something that was really sweet for me. I heard Amasa Miller playing piano for Charlie's daughter, Charmaine, at a club in New Orleans, and we just kind of clicked. I started singing with him at a bar in New Orleans when the Brothers weren't touring, with the idea that it would be a chance between gigs to let out the music that was trapped inside my heart.

Don't get me wrong, I loved playing with the Brothers and give thanks to them. They opened so many doors for me, helped me hone my skills, introduced me to so many fans. I was into the funk just as much as anybody. But I had this tender area that I wanted to share with the world—music I could whisper and it came out so pure.

Playing with Amasa gave me that outlet. We did quite a few of those dynamic duo shows in the late 1980s at a place in New Orleans called Snug Harbor, and people liked them so much that we also did a few shows in New York City, at Brooklyn's Church of St. Ann and the Holy Trinity. It's a very small church with great acoustics, and they had a cool music program there. Back then the Neville

Brothers were either touring or recording about 300 days out of 365, so I didn't get to take that duo on the road the way I would have liked. But I loved having the chance to occasionally bring that tender music into the tough world.

Around about that time I made a recording of the old Hoagy Carmichael song "Stardust" with the bass player Rob Wasserman (who has played with just about everyone, from Van Morrison to Jerry Garcia to Neil Young) for an album of duets with Rob. The first time I heard that song was on a recording by Billy Ward and His Dominoes, and Clyde McPhatter and Jackie Wilson were in that group. I wanted to do it like them, with all those layers, like the way Artie and Izzy Koo had showed me back in the Calliope Projects. So me and Rob went to Willie Nelson's studio in Austin, Texas, and I started laying down all the vocal tracks, one by one, harmonizing with myself. Willie was there, and he'd recorded "Stardust" himself in a version I loved. Willie Nelson's voice sounds like an instrument when he sings, so I was thrilled to meet him but also very nervous. Willie looked at me through the glass in the recording booth the whole time I was singing, track after track, and I could tell from his face that he was totally digging what I was doing. Him being there gave me courage.

Rob and I did the song live on David Sanborn's show called *Sunday Night*. They brought in a big old tape player with my harmonies and I sang the lead. David explained that I couldn't sing all the parts at the same time, and I said, "Next year I will."

I loved doing those quiet, intimate kinds of performances. But I had the opposite experience in the summer of 1990 when we did a two-month tour of Europe with the great Tina Turner, playing eighty thousand–plus soccer arenas. Tina had a huge show with platforms and cranes and cherry pickers and lights and pyrotechnics, and there was a lot of equipment to move around and put in place. It took more than a day to get it all set up, so they had three stages: one the show was on, one already set up at the next venue, and one on the trucks en route. That's what gave me the idea to write the song "Give the Roadies Some," watching those people climbing to the sky setting up the stage for the shows. They put in long hours and did a lot of work for not a lot of money. When people come to the show they don't see all the work that went into setting it up and what it took to get it going. None of us could have been there without the roadies.

The band on that tour was the Brothers, plus Eric Strothers on guitar, Tony Hall on bass, and Eric Kolb on keyboards. No cranes and pyrotechnics for us; we just stood on the stage and played. That's all we needed.

Those stadium concerts were outdoors, and it seemed like the sun would be shining bright when we were on, and when Tina came on it would usually start raining. All the people would brave the rain with their cigarette lighters flaming, shouting "Tina! Tina! Tina!" She put on a great show, too, rain and all.

Joel came with me on that tour, and we had a lot of fun visiting places in Italy and Spain and France. We walked up to the top of the Eifel Tower in Paris, and it looked like it was swaying all the way to the side. The promoter brought us to a play in Paris that had a big stage with a helicopter and a water tank with a submarine in it. I had never seen anything like that before. We went to that club called Moulin Rouge, too, where the girls dance the can-can.

In Milan, I sang "Ave Maria" in this huge, magnificent domed church called the Duomo di Milano. Looking up into that dome, I wondered what did they use for cranes in the 1300s to reach so high.

The next year our promoter, Bill Graham, brought us to Israel with Joe Cocker and Jack Bruce. I swam in the Mediterranean and saw where the SCUD missiles were on the beach—it was during one of the many wars in Israel. It was a cool trek to see where Jesus was born and the places where he preached. I remember being in the hotel looking out at the Sea of Galilee and realizing that Jesus walked on it. Morty Wiggins, our manager when we traveled, went with me to the Wailing Wall in Jerusalem and we prayed there together. That's something I'll never forget.

Our kids were grown by then, so Joel came with me whenever she could. But most of the time it was just me and my brothers. If we were on a bus, we'd spend a lot of time talking about our childhood and all the things we did in our younger days, the stupid stuff and the nice stuff—a lot of stupid stuff. We had some secrets that we sometimes let go on the bus.

We would be harmonizing and coming up with new songs, too, so even though it was a lot of hours, it wasn't dull. The only thing we'd argue about was what to put on the set list, but it wasn't really an argument, more like a disagreement. Other than that it was love and respect, and I was glad to be out there with them. Since we'd work out new material while we were out on the road, when we'd go into the studio to make an album we were pretty much ready.

If it was a nice bus, I kind of liked bus travel. But airports were another story. Think of all the boring, annoying things that happen to you when you fly; they happen to performers too—just more often. I call it Airport Agony: "I'm sorry but your flight was delayed and you're going to miss your connecting flight and we don't know where your luggage is going to be so good luck."

You get used to it. You've got to get into a book or listen to some music and just go along with the flow. A couple of times my suitcase got lost and I had to wear whatever I was wearing to travel onstage, but with the brothers it wasn't a dress-up thing anyway—not like back when I was wearing a tuxedo onstage. We were way past wearing the suits and the Indian regalia.

I remember once we got snowed in at O'Hare Airport in Chicago for nine hours. One of the sound guys, who we called Breeze (a.k.a. Jeffrey Gex), was with us, and he was the kind of guy who did not keep quiet. We were all sitting around at the gate, and he kept those people entertained the whole nine hours. He was just walking around talking to people, telling stories. I can't even remember what he was talking about, but he would not stop. I was sitting there praying we would get out, or else we would have had to stay there another day. Finally, we got a break and the plane could take off. Breeze wasn't quiet on the plane either. He did not stop talking.

My favorite airplane memory—although it was much later—was one time I was flying from New Orleans to Los Angeles and just happened to be sitting next to Frankie Valli from the Four Seasons. I didn't recognize him, but he recognized me. We started talking and then we started reminiscing about the songs we grew up listening to, and it was like, "You remember this one." And then we started singing. We had a big audience, the flight attendants and everybody, the whole five-hour trip. The people in the back of the plane started coming up. Somebody yelled, "I'll buy them a round of drinks," but we were in first class, so the drinks were free anyway.

The worst for flying—at least for me—was Canada. I really liked playing there, and we had some great gigs, including opening for Elton John in 2011 at Festival Quebec. It was an outdoor concert, and we played to three or four sections of two hundred thousand people, including some watching on jumbo TV screens. Also, my friend the wrestler Bret "the Hitman" Hart lived in Calgary. I got to visit him once and meet his parents. His father, Stu Hart, taught a lot of the young wrestlers down in their basement, which he called the Dungeon. The floor was covered with wrestling mats, and Stu offered to show me some moves, but I didn't want to get thrown around the ring with those guys.

What made Canada the worst for me is that every time we crossed the border, they'd take me aside and I'd be there for a couple of hours. Me and Michael Goods, our keyboard player, had a record from decades back, and they'd detain us every time. (Charles got his record expunged, so he never got pulled over.) Some guy in a uniform would come over and say, "We need to talk to you. You come over here and sit in this room." And then a couple of hours passed during which nothing happened, and then we were free to go. No doubt almost everyone did something when they were a kid that they could have been arrested for. Some got lucky and didn't get caught. For those of us who did, a record follows you all your life. Canada was the only place it happened, but we knew every time we went there we'd have to sit in the airport for a couple of hours. After a while, I never went back.

When "Everybody Plays the Fool" from my 1991 solo album, *Warm Your Heart*, hit it big in New Zealand, Australia, and Japan, Bill Graham arranged for us to tour there with Irma Thomas and Dr. John. We started out in Japan—a place I liked a lot. I remember riding the bullet train and seeing Mount Fuji off in the distance. It's someplace so famous that it feels like you're looking at a postcard or a movie backdrop. It didn't look real.

The hotel rooms in Japan were so small you couldn't even turn around in them and the television was all in Japanese. I turned it on and saw things I knew, like Popeye the Sailor Man, but he was speaking Japanese. It was pretty funny.

Even though I'm a big man and obviously not Japanese, people were so respectful. I liked how they'd bow to me and bow to each other. The people who came to our shows were really hip to the Neville Brothers. They would be waiting outside with stacks of our albums for us to sign. They didn't speak English but they knew all the words to the songs. We'd end up signing more than a hundred albums on the way out, but we sure didn't mind.

The first night we were in Tokyo, though, my back went out on me. I turned over on the bed and when I tried to turn back, my back said, "No you're not." I felt pain everywhere in my body. I rolled onto the floor, called Michael Jones, our road manager, and said, "Jonesy, come with a wheelchair and take me to the hospital."

It turned out I had a herniated disk, probably stemming from when I worked on the docks. So now I had excruciating pain up and down my thighs. They tried acupuncture, massage, everything, but nothing helped. So the doctors just gave me some Vicodin and we kept touring. "Everybody Plays the Fool" was the hit song driving the tour, and if I went home, the gigs folded.

We finished up the tour with me in a wheelchair everywhere except onstage. They'd push me into the wings and then I'd walk across the stage to a chair they'd set out for me to sit in while I sang. The sciatica was in both my legs, and it felt like they would just open up if I tried to walk, so I'd have to keep my hands on my thighs to walk from the wheelchair to the chair onstage. But I sucked it up and went on every night. After I sat down and looked at the audience and started singing, I forgot about the pain until the show was over. Then I'd feel it all over my body again.

I wish we could've been making the big money, and I wished I could have gone home. I never wanted to get paid as a headliner—whatever we got, we split even among the four of us. When I had some hit singles and the money went up, everybody still got the same across the board. So it was on me to be there and sing the songs everyone came to hear.

On that tour, we ended in New Zealand, where my song hit number one. I am so glad we went there, even with all that pain all over my body. It was a very special place for me. The Maori people met us at the airport and did a dance where they held spears and stomped the ground and stuck their tongues out—a way to show their passion and ferocity. The Moahunters sang a Maori hymn,

"Whakaaria Mai," which is "How Great Thou Art," and we joined in with them in English. A TV crew recorded it all, and it still brings tears of joy to my eyes whenever I hear it. The next year we invited Moana and the Moahunters to come to New Orleans and play the Jazz Fest, and the crowd loved them.

The good memories about that trip outweigh the bad—and I could say that about all my time on the road with my brothers. But I've saved the sweetest memory for last. It was in 1986 and we played the Montreux Jazz Festival. The founder of the festival, Claude Nobs, invited us to hang out at his chalet high in the mountains. Our tour bus brought us up there with the whole band. We'd be going around these winding roads, and you'd be looking down and you couldn't see nothing, knowing that if the bus turned over it would be a long ways down. It was kind of like when I was fighting those fires in California where the wheels were coming off the road and you were just looking at it.

Claude's chalet had the best view overlooking the Alps, and we just lay in some lounge chairs and took it all in. You might be thinking that's a long way from when I used to stay in guesthouses with Larry Williams's valet and shinny down the drainpipe so we didn't have to pay the bill. You might be thinking that's very far away from the Calliope. No doubt. But that's not what I was thinking.

I was just absorbing all the fine scenery and realizing that I'm up here with my brothers and we're all doing what we were born to do. We'd all taken a hard journey to get there—drugs, jails, all kinds of adversity. But this was our calling. We were exactly where we were supposed to be.

17

The End of the Ritual

Like I said before, using heroin is not just about the dope itself, it's about the ritual, and a drug addict loves all of it. You love the danger of going to score, the possibility of getting busted; you love the sight and feel of the needle going into your vein, seeing the blood register in the syringe. You even love the withdrawal somehow—the hustle is part of it. The addiction is to the whole ritual. You fall in love with it. But it's not in love with you. It's going to betray you in the end. That ritual had cost me so much—damn near cost me everything a couple of times.

We made a deal with A&M Records to record *Fiyo on the Bayou* in New York in 1981. Bette Midler helped us with that deal after she heard the Neville Brothers play a gig at Tipitina's. She slid right off her stool when I sang "Tell It Like It Is," then called Jerry Moss and Herb Alpert at A&M.

That's when I knew I really had to clean up my act. I was fighting for my life. I knew that if I didn't kick for good, it would take me out. When we were out on the road, me, Cyril, and Charles did heroin together (Artie only did a little coke). Looking to score added to the exhaustion of touring, but we were all caught up in the game. A lot of times we'd try to be sober for a minute, but then we'd be right back on the horse. We called it the rat race, and that's just what it was.

I was really tired of running. I drew a picture of myself on a cross with syringes as the nails. It was killing me slowly. I was ready to kick for good. I decided after we finished recording that album, I wanted to go to rehab. My manager, Bill Johnston, set it up for me at DePaul Hospital in New Orleans, which used to be a hospital for the insane. That was fitting, I guess, because I sure had seen a lot of insanity. I brought enough dope up to New York with me to last for the recording session, and I decided after that I'd be done.

I was excited and afraid. I knew what it was to be in the game. I knew what mainlining did to me. I knew what withdrawal feels like. But begging off the drugs entirely—that was a new venture. I was forty years old, and I hadn't been clean since junior high school.

It was hard for me to sleep at night. We were staying at a friend's apartment, and they had a Wurlitzer set up in the room, so I'd sit at the electric piano at three in the morning and sing spirituals by Sam Cooke and the Soul Stirrers. I first heard their song "Any Day Now I'm Going to Heaven" when I was thirteen years old, and I always knew that I wanted to sing those songs. Whenever Artie knew I was going through changes, he'd give me a tape of Sam Cooke and the Soul Stirrers and it would calm me somewhat.

That night, the little kid in me went all the way back to sixth grade at St. Monica's Catholic School, when I had to stand in front of the class and recite the poem "Lovely Lady Dressed in Blue, Teach Me How to Pray." I started making it into a song, as if someone was telling me how it should go. It ended up on my 1997 album, *To Make Me Who I Am*, and what's on the record is how it came out that night—from the scared little kid in me.

I sang for hours. I had borrowed my friend John Brenes's cassette recorder, and he still has the tapes I made that night. You can hear every emotion in my voice: the fear, the hope, and everything in between. I was crying and laughing at the same time. It was a long, dark night.

Recording *Fiyo on the Bayou* was an amazing experience. I already said that a lot of producers tried to take us to their idea of how our music should go, but Joel Dorn did the opposite on *Fiyo on the Bayou*: He brought that same fire out of us that you hear on the live albums. Keith Richards said in a *Rolling Stone* interview that he thought it was the best album of the year, and I agree. Seventeen-year-old Whitney Houston and her mom, Cissy, sang backing vocals on that album, and an a capella group from Brooklyn, the Persuasions, did the background vocals for me on "The Ten Commandments of Love." Plus I recorded "Mona Lisa," my all-time favorite Nat King Cole song—the one I used to pretend I was performing back when I was a kid.

To arrange the strings on "Mona Lisa," A&M brought in Leon Pendarvis, a string player from the *Saturday Night Live* band, and Wardell Quezergue, an arranger and producer from New Orleans who had worked with Toussaint and Sehorn. The idea was that the orchestra would play both arrangements, and then we'd decide which one was best.

The producer asked Wardell if he needed a piano in his hotel room, and he said, "No, I just need a tuning fork." That's the way he wrote charts—he was a genius. But I could see the New York string players snickering at Wardell like he was a country bumpkin.

When the time came, the orchestra played Leon's chart first; it was way cool. Then they played Wardell's chart, and when they finished, they had to stand up and tap their bows on their music stands to give him his props. (That's how string players applaud.) I had tears in my eyes when I heard that arrangement.

I dedicated "Mona Lisa" to my mother and father, and asked for their prayers and blessings. The song sounded magnificent, and after I recorded it I felt at peace. I was ready for a new start, a new way of life. No more ripping and running, peeping and dodging police cars. I was like a worm getting ready to turn into a butterfly.

When we finished the album I went straight home and Joel took me to the rehab center. No turning back now. I knew that if I didn't do it I would probably OD.

There was every kind of person there in rehab—rich and poor, Black and white. For the first ten days I wasn't allowed to talk to anyone on the outside, and that was really hard, but after that I called Joel every day and she came to see me a couple of times. They gave me some medicine to help me through the physical withdrawal, but I'd been doing cold turkey on and off for years. I remember back the last time I was on my way to New York, I ended up lying down underneath the back seat of the bus to get comfortable between throwing up in the john, until I could score again. The physical aspects of Mr. Jones were not the worst part for me.

I think the worst part was that I didn't know how to be a grown-up in the grown-up world I was living in. I'd been using for so long that whenever anything got to me, the only way I knew how to handle it was to do up and nod out. I just didn't know how to *be* if I wasn't being a junkie.

After I was there about a week, this elderly white lady said to me, "Aaron, when you first came in here I was afraid of you. But since then I've seen your heart. You have a good soul." Then she handed me a book called *The Greatest Miracle in the World*, by Og Mandino. She said, "My daughter gave me this book and it's helped me tremendously."

That book felt like it was burning in my hands, and I couldn't wait to get back to my room and read it. It was a story about this guy named Simon Potter. He called himself the rag picker, and he would try to rescue lost souls on the streets. The more I read, the more I was thinking, "Is this character really Jesus?" At the end of the book was a section called Memorandum from God to You. It explained how you were a miracle; how when your mother and father made love and conceived you, there were millions of cells fighting for a chance, but only one made it, and that was you. You made it through those odds while all the rest of them gave up the ghost. And then you came out—your special, one-in-a-couple-of-millions self.

When I read that, it really made me start looking at myself and others differently. I read that book every day for two hundred days, until the idea got deep into my subconscious. I am a miracle. If you've heard me in interviews, you've probably heard me say it. I believe I am a miracle. I believe you are. Something big changed in me.

I learned a couple of other important things in rehab, too, like how drugs mess up your internal organs. I was still thinking like a sixteen-year-old, and what I learned was some scary shit. The dope was attacking my liver and my kidneys, and I realized, "Wow, so that's what that feeling was!" You feel it in your midsection—especially the Ts and blues hit you in your organs. So you end up destroying yourself from the inside. Plus you're blowing out your veins. When I learned about what I was doing to my body, that was enough right there to make me want to quit.

Remember, this was before AIDS, so junkies were not yet dying because they got it from sharing needles. What you heard about on the news, and what we knew about on the streets, was people dying of overdoses. But plenty more died from just running their bodies down until they couldn't take it anymore.

I thought about my old friend and junko partner Rooney. He and me did the Ts and blues together. We used to talk about getting clean, but we were still dabbling then. Rooney hadn't been feeling well, so I would tell him to go to the hospital. He'd say, "Okay, Red, I'm gonna go," but when he finally went, it was too late and he never came home. His organs failed. I didn't want that to be me. I realized I could save my life by making different choices.

They also told us in rehab that what you're doing to your body and your mind doesn't just affect you. It affects your family and everyone around you. I'd spent a long time telling myself that because I was never catching and nodding at home, my family was out of it. When she left me, Joel made it clear she thought otherwise. Now, finally, I guess I had grown up enough that it sunk in.

The other side of that, though, is that when you do something wrong, it will only be you living the aftermath of it. Yes, it affects other people, but no one else will live your reality. If you're in jail, you're the only one in jail—not your parents or your friends, only you. If you get addicted to drugs, you're the only one who will feel the euphoria and the pain. It's a personal thing. Wherever you go, there you are, by yourself.

I also realized that my habit was all on me. I had been hearing about heroin since the Calliope Projects and I wanted to do it. Charles tried to talk me out of it, but I insisted. In rehab I heard a lot of people talking about heredity and how everyone in their family had been addicts for generations. All I inherited from my family was my music. I heard some people talking about terrible abuse from the people in their lives and how they turned to drugs to escape it. I didn't have any of that. I had to own my habit, all by myself. I loved the excitement and the ritual. I was inquisitive and I wanted to do it.

My inquisitive nature ultimately took me to some beautiful places. I sang songs in just about every genre, with just about every kind of singer from Pavarotti to Ernie on *Sesame Street*. It took me down that brighter path, but it also took me down this darker path. I could not own one without owning the other. It was all on me and I took my rap. I wanted to take responsibility for my life in a way I hadn't before—be the father, husband, person I was meant to be.

Rehab was supposed to be four weeks, but I wasn't ready to go yet, so I stayed two more weeks. My whole family was excited for me to come home. The kids knew where I was and thought it was fabulous. And I was a different person. It felt great to not have that want or desire for the dope anymore. I was ready for a new adventure of walking the straight and narrow. My eyes were clear, my voice was at its peak, it was a whole new world for me.

One of the rules they tell you in rehab is that you have to stop hanging out with the bad guys. So when I came out, I had to change friends and keep my running buddies at bay. I tried to stay close to home until I could get my footing in a life without drugs. I used to just hang out on my front porch and harmonize with some of my neighbors, like Philip and Terry Manuel and my boy Barry Trudeaux, or do things with Joel and the kids. I had started feeling good about myself, and I wouldn't let anything turn that around.

When me and my brothers were on the road, I was the junkie police. If I saw any shady characters around, I told them, "Get to stepping, sucker!" Cyril and Charles weren't quite ready to quit yet, but I believe by me making the move, it inspired them to also want to get off the horse. You've got to remember that a junkie won't get out of it unless they're ready. You can't do it for anyone else. Cyril was next to go into rehab, and Charlie went about a year later up in Eugene, Oregon, and stayed for almost a year but finally got clean.

An old friend of ours, James Booker, who I call the piano prince, didn't make it through. He comes to mind when I think about rehab and all the paths me and my brothers could have taken. He must've started playing piano and organ as soon as he was born—he was playing Bach when he was a little kid. He went to St. Monica's Catholic School with me and Charles and Artie, and to Xavier Prep with Joel, so we got to be real close.

When he was just ten, he got hit by an ambulance on Galvez Street, not far from school, and got dragged all the way down the street. His leg was never right after that, but he eventually came back to school and was still a piano genius. I remember reading a story in the newspaper about how Booker played for the great concert pianist Arthur Rubenstein when he was eighteen years old and Rubenstein said, "I could never play that . . . never at that tempo."

Booker said the morphine they gave him for the pain started him on his jones. He ended up in and out of jail, and he got to know the DA, Harry Connick Sr.—who knocked down his sentence in exchange for Booker teaching his son, Harry Connick Jr., how to play the piano. Booker and Charles met up in Angola, and he was in Charlie's prison band along with the drummer James Black, Morris Bachemin on sax (who was an original member of Artie's band, the Hawketts), and Smiling George from the Calliope Projects on vocals. All were hard hitters at the bat, and that was one funky band.

Booker would do all kinds of crazy things. At some point in the early 1970s he lost an eye. He told all kinds of wild stories about how it happened, but nobody really knew the truth. Dr. John described him as "the best Black, gay, one-eyed junkie piano genius New Orleans has ever produced." Sometimes he would come in from Europe, where he was well respected, to New Orleans, where he wasn't much appreciated. He came to visit me and Joel on Valence Street sometimes when he was in town. He'd take a taxi and would tell the driver to keep the meter running, and he would play our piano for two to three hours. I would be mesmerized watching him, because he sounded like he had four hands; his left hand could do the same as his right hand.

He had a wicked dope habit. I remember he recorded an old New Orleans song called "Junco Partner." The lyrics say I want whiskey when I'm frisky and heroin before I die. But when Booker sang it, he said he wanted heroin long before he died, and a little cocaine on the side.

Sometimes he would check himself into the psych ward at the charity hospital, and they would let him stay there until he felt better. Joel worked at the charity hospital in the billing department, so she would go and visit him there. One time she was ready to leave and she was waving at the guard outside, and the guard started waving back at her like she was one of the patients. He got a good taste of her potty mouth then.

From what Dr. John told me, it was the dope man who drove Booker to the charity hospital after he OD'd, pushed him into the emergency room, and left him here. He sat there in a wheelchair and died—nobody knew who he was. Booker was just forty-four. That was in 1983. I read later that he died not from the OD but from kidney failure after all that dope.

To all my addicted brothers and sisters, believe me, I know what you're going through. I've been there and done that. I know how it started out to be such a great feeling, and it tricks you into thinking that it's gonna be your good friend. Yes, it'll be your friend for a while, then it will turn on you with a vengeance, drag you through the bowels of hell with gasoline drawers on.

Addiction is a lonely and personal journey. No one can feel the pain and agony that you feel. All the lonely, sick days and nights belong only to you. And until you realize that it's not your friend at all, it's really the devil in disguise, it will ruin your life, your family's lives, and anyone around you. And then it will take your life.

I hope and pray, for all who are struggling, that somehow you find a way to save your precious lives. Remember that God loves you, so love yourself. I don't know much, but I know I love you.

18

It Wasn't All Craziness

My life changed one hundred percent after rehab. Finally, I knew who I was and had learned how to love myself. I'd turned totally around. After spending so many years chasing my habit, all I wanted to do was give back, try to make up for some of the wrong things I'd done. Even with my singing, I felt like God was letting me use His voice in a new way to help put back some tenderness in a rough, coarse world. Singing has always been medicine to me, and I decided I would try to administer it all around and tenderize the world.

I had a lot more energy and a lot more time—both of which I'd been using up ripping and running for so long. And after so much craziness, I knew for sure I wanted to do something for my community. Every block in New Orleans is my stomping ground, and I care a lot about what happens there—always have.

The idea of a community center was in the air; anyone I talked to said it was needed. I guess it was written in the stars to happen—for sure it was something I wanted to do, and I prayed for it. I used to see young kids in my neighborhood, even my own kids, hanging out on the street with nothing to do. I wanted to give them a place that offered another direction, a way to steer clear of that dope fiend shit, a chance to hang out someplace safe and fun.

And it turned out that a lot of people wanted to help. I knew the mayor, Dutch Morial (the first Black mayor of New Orleans), because I did a benefit concert for him when he was trying to get elected. He was a really cool, down-to-earth guy, and he was definitely into the idea.

The mayor let us use an abandoned firehouse on Laurel and Upperline Streets in the Thirteenth Ward, and Murphy Oil, a Louisiana company, gave us a grant to fix it up, plus we raised some money doing concerts with local New Orleans musicians—Irma Thomas, Clarence Frogman Henry, the Neville Brothers (of course!), and a few others. We painted the center purple, gold, and green—the colors of New Orleans. It was definitely cool. Not what you'd expect.

I was friends with a lot of people in New Orleans, and got them all together to get things running. Sister Jane Remson took care of the benefit part of the program, Lynne Batson and attorney Alan Tusa did the legal work, and Mayor Morial helped me to get it all worked out. It was the start of the Uptown Youth Center. Our friend Al Alonzo, who was a paraplegic, was the head of the center. He had a motorized wheelchair and could get around just fine. We even put in an elevator so Al could get upstairs, where we had classrooms.

The Uptown Youth Center opened up in 1982 to all the kids of New Orleans. We had boys and girls, all ages, Black, brown, white, Asian. That was the coolest thing about it. Those kids just wanted someplace safe to be and something to do, and they managed to figure out on their own how to be doing that together.

Anything you could have in that kind of community center, we did it. There was afterschool tutoring, arts and crafts, dancing, and Mardi Gras Indian sewing workshops. And because the Nevilles were involved, there were music lessons. Sometimes musicians would stop by and show the kids how they played their instruments. We had a choir, too, and the kids would put on concerts and plays for people in the community to come see what they were doing. The mayor even used to stop by from time to time.

The Wisner Playground was right across the street, so the kids could play baseball, football, and other sports. We had groups for different ages, plus a place for the little kids to just run around. Joel had been a teacher's aide, and she helped with some of the classes. Aaron Jr. (a.k.a. Fred) knew so much about sports that he could have been a sportscaster, so he helped out with the teams. There were all size kids there—small size, middle size, and a little more grown—and all my kids helped out with the little ones.

The center was right around the corner from my house, and I'd stop by every day to play ball and talk to the kids. I'd always tell them to try to be the best person you can be, and talk to them about what drugs can do to your health and your family. When I'm saying it now, I know it sounds kind of stiff, but it wasn't like that. Those kids listened to people who they thought were sincere. They respected me because I was honest about what I did, and they knew that I'd changed things up and turned my life around.

Some needed more talking than others. It was like when I looked down the street, I'd see a bunch of flowers, but some kids would just see a pile of trash. I sometimes had to pull a kid aside and say, "Hey, man, what do you want in life? Do you even know?" And that gets us way back to what I said about me and my brothers having something we were working for, a reason to get through the struggle. I always knew what I wanted to do and where I wanted to go. Sometimes I took the detour, but I always had that picture in my mind. But when there's nothing you want to struggle for, you can fall into grabbing for anything.

There was this one little guy named Freddie who used to sit on my porch on Valence Street. He wore this gold chain around his neck, and one day a guy took it off him. Freddie told me, "I got to go do him."

I said, "Is that gold chain worth your life now?"

He said, "I can't let it go. It's the principle of the thing; he took my chain and I got to take him out."

I said, "I know it, but a word to the wise is sufficient." When I was a kid, I didn't really get what that meant, but I did by then. Freddie, though, he killed that dude and did twenty years in prison. For a gold chain. When you've got nothing but a little bit of gold and a lot of pride, it's hard to look ahead to where that shit will take you.

I knew how easy it was to get in trouble and how hard it was to get out of trouble. With that in mind, we decided to charter some buses and take the kids, the girls and the boys, up to the Louisiana State Penitentiary at Angola to talk to some of the prisoners, like scared straight.

During those visits we made friends with a couple of lifers, including Wilbert Rideau, who'd spent twelve years in solitary on death row. He'd used that time to read books and educate himself, and when his sentence was changed to life, he ended up editing the prison newspaper, *The Angolite*. He sometimes published my poems in the paper, and I was on the mailing list, so I got it at home. (I'll tell you more about my poetry in a little bit.) Wilbert was an amazing dude, and when he finally got out after a retrial, he started writing books and making documentary films. Wilbert and some of the other prisoners would talk to the kids and say straight up that Angola is a place you do not want to be at. Kids don't think about the consequences of what they do, so we all were hoping this kind of experience would get them thinking a little deeper.

I know we helped a lot of them. But not all. I remember years later the Neville Brothers played a concert at Angola and a young man approached me. The guard raised his gun like he wanted to shoot the guy, but I asked the guard to let him talk with me. He said, "Mr. Neville, you brought me up here in 1982 to see this place. Now I'm back up here with fifty years inside." My heart sank for him, because fifty years in Angola meant exactly that—fifty years. People didn't get out early. He was going to die there, probably. My heart was sick. I realized some are saved and some fall by the wayside.

The other side of it was that a lot of people over the years have come up to me and said thank you for the Uptown Youth Center because it helped them stay away from all the dope and the gang stuff going on around them. Some told me they believed it saved their lives. The center was open for about ten years, and I know for sure it did a lot of good. Plenty of kids just grew up and are living ordinary lives, which is why you don't necessarily see the good that was done. And I'm fine with that.

One thing I really didn't expect that happened around this time is that I made friends with some police officers. I used to go back to the parish prison sometimes to sing for the guys inside, and I got to be friendly with some of the officers there. They heard about the Uptown Youth Center and would come by to play ball with the kids. These were different kinds of cops from when I was a kid. When I was growing up the police would come in the neighborhoods to show you they were the boss. And you had to do what they said. You couldn't even stand on the sidewalk, or you'd get arrested for something stupid like loitering.

Back in the 1990s, Artie told me he ran into one of the worst cops from our old neighborhood. He was a little short guy who everybody called Turtle, and I think he must have had a Napoleon complex. Turtle used to mess with me every time he saw me. He'd come out popping his fingers and say stuff like, "Oh, the rock and roll singer. You know you're going to jail." One time I was sitting on my mother's steps, and he came around in his patrol car and said, "Aaron, come in the car."

I said, "What am I going to jail for?"

The blue(s) men. We closed out Jazz Fest for more than twenty years, until 2013, when we turned over that honor to Trombone Shorty.

I love this poster. The artist, James Michalopoulos, really captured my soul.

Me and my brother Cyril, a.k.a. the Ratty Chin. Cyril was the militant one, but you had to be, the way we were pushed.

Me and my lifelong friend the good Dr. John (a.k.a. Mac Rebennack), relaxicating for the last time in 2016 at my seventy-fifth birthday celebration at Brooklyn Bowl. I know he's playing in the heavenly orchestra with Artie and Charlie and a bunch more. RIP, Mac.

My living room in the Eastover subdivision of New Orleans, in the house that Hurricane Katrina took from us. That piano was flattened and nothing was left. I never went back to that house, but I saw pictures of it all.

Me and George Jones, one of my favorite country singers. I asked him why they called him the Possum, and he said, "Well hell, I look like a damn possum."

Me and Paul Simon and Wynton Marsalis hanging out at Lincoln Center in 2012 after a concert called the Paul Simon Songbook. I sang "Bridge Over Troubled Water" and "Take Me to the Mardi Gras."

Willie Nelson—they called him the Redheaded Stranger. We were on his tour bus in LA, where we stepped out to take a picture. We were all in town for the 2015 concert where Bob Dylan was honored as the MusiCares Person of the Year. I have much love and respect for Bob.

Me and Carlos Santana around 20[ ] at Jazz Fest. We used to call each o[ ] brothers, because Santana and the Neville Brothers did a lot of shows together. There was respect all the [ ] around.

Me and Keith Richards got to be friends. We give each other a shout-out on each of our birthdays, and he ended up coproducing *My True Story*. Another brother from another mother.

Me and my quintet opened for Elton Joh[ ] in Quebec in 2011. He was a nice guy, ar[ ] I'd been a big fan of his for a long time, s[ ] it was an honor to share the stage.

Linda Ronstadt and me get our Grammys in 1991. When I walked out there to sing with her, my nerves were like wildfire, looking at all the famous people in the audience. I almost tripped over a wire coming out from behind the curtain. My nerves didn't calm down until I was there looking in Linda's eyes. I never took my eyes off her for the whole song.

It was great honor to be celebrating my dear friend Linda Ronstadt at the Kennedy Center Honors in 2019. I sang "I Don't Know Much" with Trisha Yearwood—with whom I also won a Grammy for the song "I Fall to Pieces."

Me and President Bill Clinton in the Oval Office in 1993. Me and Linda sang at Clinton's inauguration in 1993 and again at a special concert. My jacket is by Manuel of Nashville, who made clothes for guys like Johnny Cash and Elvis. It was an honor meeting President Clinton; I shook his hand, and he felt human.

In 2006 I sang at the White House again when George and Laura Bush gave a state dinner for the National Governors' Association meeting. Laura told me I was her favorite singer.

Courtesy of Sarah A. Friedman

My nickname from way back. My dog is Little Apache.

I had this license plate on a few cars, including my Ford Thunderbird, the first car that I bought brand-new. It wasn't stolen.

Courtesy of Sarah A. Friedman

In 2009 Sarah came up to Ango with me and made a film of me singing and talking with the inmates. The cell here is on Dea Row, and back in the day this could have been me.

Pumping iron; I first got into it at Camp 18 Forestry Camp in California when I was doing time for burglary.

Me and my trainer Andrie (a.k.a Drago) in New York. He's a great trainer. I still talk with him. Now me and Sarah work out together and keep each other strong. I love it!

I married Sarah, my fourth and last angel, in 2010; this is a picture from our wedding. A very happy day in my life.

Me and my little bitty buddy Apache. When me and Sarah got him, he stole our hearts and he still possesses them.

Turks and Caicos are our two rescue cats. Turks likes to lie on my chest and look deep into my eyes, like she knows me.

Me and Sarah on Freville Farm in 2022, being happy.

He said, "I'll think of something by the time we get to the precinct."

Me and my brothers tried not to take any shit from the police, not act like we were scared of them or owed them any respect. They just kept after guys like us, trying to bully you into submission. Anyway, Artie said Turtle told him, "Tell your brother Aaron I'm sorry for how I treated him. We were all young men back then."

I thought, "Too late to tell me you're sorry, after you ran my ass ragged back then with all those seventy-two hours in the precinct." We were all young men, but we are all still responsible for what we did. I own my mistakes. What about you?

Through Artie, I met Johnny Miller, a homicide detective. Johnny was a friend of the actor John Goodman, who loved New Orleans and used to spend a lot of time there. John Goodman got to know Artie, and introduced him to Johnny.

The woman who used to help Joel clean our house was friends with a policewoman named Debbie Prevost, who hung out with the singers in the Dixie Cups. Debbie would come by sometimes, and I got to be friends with her, too.

The cops I made friends with, Debbie and Johnny and the others, actually helped me get a license to carry a gun and brought me to the shooting range to learn how to use it safely. New Orleans was getting crazy in the early 1980s, with carjackings and all that, and I was driving that great big T-bird. So I kept the gun under me on the seat when I went out at night. I thank God I never had to use it.

As I got more involved in community work, I got to meet the chief of police, Marlin Gusman, who made me an honorary officer. I helped some judges by doing benefit concerts for their campaigns, and I helped Richard Ieyoub become Louisiana's attorney general. I even met Governor Edwin Edwards—who eventually helped me out when my son Jason got into trouble. I spoke with all of these guys personally, and they seemed like real down-to-earth, honest people, which is why I chose to support them. I'm still friends with all of them, and I believe they have done some good in New Orleans.

I've been arrested more times than I rightly remember, a lot of times for things I didn't do (although sometimes for things I did). So this wasn't exactly how I expected my relationship with the law would go. But the fact is that I have a New Orleans Sherriff's Department badge, plus one from the Jefferson Parish Sheriff's Department (given to me by Sheriff Harry Lee), and a Special Agent badge from the Louisiana State Police that Richard Ieyoub and Fran LaSalle (the head of the state police) gave me. They were all given to me and Artie because we were doing things to try to help kids stay out of trouble and grow up easier. And those badges do mean something to me. They make me think about my days gone by—who I was and where I come from and who I am now.

Some people are talking about the police now like maybe we shouldn't even have police. I think that's crazy. I've met a lot of police in my time and some are good and some are not. I'm sure in every city there's police who've done some bad things, but you can't charge every police officer with what a small percentage of assholes have done. I try to take each one for the person they are. If you're going to be an asshole like Turtle, I can't forgive you for what you did. But if you're going to be a good person, we can work together—and we can be friends.

Right after rehab was a time in my life when I was doing a lot of soul cleansing. I know that God had been walking with me and brought me safe to the other side. I remember each time He carried me. Me and Joel were really happy. We were still living on Valence Street, the Neville Brothers played a lot in New Orleans, at Tipitina's, Jimmy's Bar, Jed's Nite Club, the Tulane University quad, and on a paddleboat in the Mississippi called the *President*. Joel would go to all the gigs, along with my sister Athelgra. We were touring, too, and Joel went on quite a few trips with us.

Ivan was about twenty-two years old, and he was gigging with us when he wasn't doing his own thing with his band. Fred was twenty, Ernestine was nineteen, and Jason was eleven. We did a lot of family things together, like visiting Joel's parents in Pontchartrain Park and going to the beach and drive-in movies. Sometimes we'd just go for a ride and play games in the car. We'd still go crabbing in my big T-bird and take a picnic lunch with us. We were just a big, goofy family—me being the biggest kid of all. We were enjoying life at last. I had finally slayed the dragon I'd been chasing for all those years.

Me and Joel were going to church a lot too. I'd sing at St. Jude's Shrine in Our Lady of Guadalupe Church, sometimes at midnight mass or at the St. Jude Novenas. It wasn't that I'd found God; He'd been beside me all along. It was more like now I was paying attention to Him.

I was still reading *The Greatest Miracle in the World* and I would buy copies and give them to family and friends who I thought could

use them. It felt good doing things to help others. I had seen enough
and felt enough for everybody.

In January 1984 it was me and Joel's twenty-fifth anniversary.
Her sister Betinna worked at a roofing company and they were taking everyone on a cruise, and Betinna invited Joel to go with her.
Joel said it might be the only chance she'd ever get to go on a cruise,
so I told her to go and I stayed home with the kids.

One night I was lying in bed thinking of her, missing her so bad
that I was aching in my whole body, and I looked out the window
and the moon was all big and yellow. I thought, "Oh wow, are you
trying to tell me something?" And I wrote a poem called "Yellow
Moon."

> *Yellow moon, yellow moon,*
> *why you keep peeping in my window?*
> *Do you know something I don't know?*
> *Did you see my baby*
> *walking down the railroad tracks?*
> *You can tell me if the girl's*
> *ever coming back.*

That poem came into my head with a kind of music swaying
around it. I knew good things were going to come of it. I had a tune
and a rhythm for it already when I wrote it, and I showed my brothers what I had in mind, and they brought it and made it into a song.
I gave Joel a writing credit on "Yellow Moon" because her great big
love is what created it.

Sometimes late at night me and Joel would watch wrestling on TV. They'd have these long commercials where they'd show little babies in Africa who were starving, with big swollen bellies and flies all around them. It made me cry. The thing is, hunger has no vaccine. And it can touch anyone. We all have stomachs that growl when we're hungry. If I'm just a little hungry, I know how much that hurts—so I tried to imagine what those little babies were feeling deep in their stomachs. It seemed so horrible. I asked God to help them, but I wanted to help too.

I told Joel that I wanted to try and do something for them. She said, "How do you know they would get the money you sent to them? We have a lot of hungry and homeless people right here in New Orleans." She got me thinking that we should do something here at home.

And around the same time I was thinking that, Allen Toussaint was thinking the same thing. There were a lot of homeless people in New Orleans—some were living in a tent city under the Claiborne Overpass. And a lot more were hungry, but you couldn't see it.

That was 1985, the year the song "We Are the World" came out to raise money to fight hunger in Africa. Me and Allen decided to start our efforts in New Orleans with our own song, "Give Today for Tomorrow," written by Allen, Sid Berger, and Alan Huard. We got a group of people together at Sea-Saint Studios to record it, including me and Allen, Irma Thomas, Frogman Henry, Frankie Ford, Pete Fountain, the Dixie Cups, the Aubrey Twins, Leigh Lil Queenie Harris, Al Carnival Time Johnson, Oliver Morgan, and a lot of others.

The song was meant to raise awareness and inspire people to help out. The real work was done by the organization we started, New Orleans Artists Against Hunger and Homelessness (NOAHH). Our main way to raise money was a bunch of benefit concerts that we ended up doing every year. Pretty much every musician in New Orleans has gotten involved in at least one of them—including, of course, the Neville Brothers. One thing about the New Orleans music scene is all you have to do is give someone a call and they're there. People are always willing to share their talent to help out wherever they can.

My old friend Sister Jane Remson became the president of NOAHH (a job she held for twenty-five years) and helped us figure out where the money should go. Our other friends Lynne Batson and attorney Alan Tusa helped out getting it going. The money always goes to small, local groups that are out in the streets of New Orleans taking care of people one-on-one. The board members are unpaid volunteers, so whatever we take in goes right to help people.

Between me and Allen, we know a lot of musicians, so over the years Huey Lewis, Rita Coolidge, Albert Finney, John Goodman, Nicolas Cage, Woody Harrelson, Emmylou Harris, Stephen Stills, Joan Baez, Dr. John, Paul Simon, Jimmy Page, Robert Plant, and Jimmy Buffett have performed at NOAHH benefits. Sometimes they donate memorabilia and it's auctioned off.

Those concerts are still going on today, even though Allen is gone and I'm retired. COVID shut them down for a couple of years, but they're back on now. I'm sad to say the need is still there, but so is the willingness to help. I set something in motion that I'm pretty sure is going to outlive me, and it's a great feeling to know that I've been able to give something back.

Late in the 1980s, the Neville Brothers started doing concerts up at Angola, too. When Charles was in prison there back in the 1960s, he'd started a music school in Angola, and he still went up there sometimes to talk to the inmates. You'd think it would be tough for him reliving those hard times, but he actually looked forward to going there so he could give back. When I met Wilbert Rideau, he told me the prisoners at Angola felt lonely and abandoned. I knew what it felt like to be pulled away from the people you care about, and it really got to me. So we arranged for the Neville Brothers to do a concert. If the warden is cool with it, it's not hard to arrange.

I actually got to be friends with the Angola warden, Burl Cain. I like him because he brought the church into Angola, to give the prisoners a reason to do things differently. At one time Angola was the bloodiest penitentiary in the country, and Warden Cain helped change that. He said men in prison need to have some kind of moral change, and part of that is seeing that there are people who care about you. Me and my brothers going up there to perform and taking the time to talk to the prisoners and hang out with them was one way to do that.

I've done a bunch of concerts at Angola, with my brothers, with other artists, and on my own. I still talk to Warden Cain, too— he's the commissioner of the Mississippi Department of Corrections now.

In 2000 I did a concert up there and made a DVD that was part of *Devotion*, my album of spiritual songs. In the DVD, Warden

Cain said that the hardest thing is to give hope where there is no hope. One way to do that is to give people opportunities to show that they could change—even though 85 percent of the inmates at Angola were likely to be there until they died. He told me about how when a prisoner was executed, he held his hand as he died and told him, "You're going to see Jesus Christ." And then he said something that's really stuck with me: "If God can forgive that horrible, horrible murder, how do we not forgive each other?"

One time I was up there and the warden was giving me a tour around the penitentiary (which includes eighteen thousand acres of farmland). We turned a corner and there was Big Snooks, my old running buddy, outside cutting another inmate's hair. I remembered Snooks as a big, strong man, but the penitentiary had worn him out. He was younger than me, but he looked much older. I immediately said to myself, "Wow! There go I but for the grace of God."

When I saw Snooks there, I knew in my heart that God had run interference for me, starting from the time He saved me from going to San Quentin in 1963, then Angola in 1965, and the federal penitentiary in 1975. I felt so bad, thinking of all the times it seemed like I had been trying to get to prison back in the day. When I was a young man, prison time was like a status thing. But God and St. Jude were there for me every time, keeping me safe despite my insisting on stupid.

In the DVD we made for *Devotion*, Snooks talked about how our lives had gone in different directions. He said, "Aaron and I attended Samuel Green Junior High School together. We identified with some of the same things—friends, girls, the things that youngsters do to make a day. Aaron had a knack for singing. He and I stayed tight a long time, but Aaron wanted to pursue something bigger, and he succeeded in getting ahold of his dream. Me, I had a taste for nice things, but I went about the wrong way of getting them. I got into crookery. And this is the result."

Snooks did forty years in Angola for armed robbery, got out about 2013, and died a year later. Nobody's health is good in prison. The food, the work, the stress—it all takes a toll on you mentally and physically. It wore down Melvin, too.

His first time in Angola was two years for car theft back when he was eighteen. Then, when we were in our twenties and really into the heroin, Melvin was selling a bag here and a bag there to support his habit. He got busted for being a heroin dealer, and the judge sentenced him to life. They'd just changed the law, and he was the first to get that sentence. But he appealed, and another judge took the life sentence back and gave him five years. He saw that Melvin wasn't a big-time dealer.

Melvin told me when he got that life sentence, it was the first time he felt fear. He didn't want to be buried in Point Lookout, the Angola graveyard.

Every time he got out, we'd hook up together. But Melvin could not stay out of trouble and ended up in and out of Angola four times. After he got out the last time in the early 1990s, he stepped off a curb and his thighbone just popped. He said it sounded like a shotgun. It broke like that because he didn't get the nourishment his bones needed all those years. He was in a cast for a year and a half. Then his blood pressure went crazy. I was doing okay at the time, so

I was trying to help him get his teeth fixed, but his pressure wouldn't get down low enough for the dentist to do what he needed done. Not long after, in 1995, he died from an aneurysm.

Melvin was one of a kind, and we were closer than brothers. As I write this book, so many of my other friends—Poochie, Stackolee, Lil Bobby, Rooney—are all gone. But they're also still with me. Sometimes I can hear a song or just a note and one of them will pass through my mind.

One of the ones who made it was Don Hubbard, the school friend I chased down in the Ford at that Abita Springs picnic that ended with me getting arrested. The same year my teacher told me I was a waste of protoplasm, Don was voted least likely to succeed. He ended up starting the largest 100 percent Black-owned and -operated services company in America, Superdome Services, brought the Ali–Spinks fight to the Superdome, and is a prominent businessman and civil rights leader in New Orleans. Kids do stupid things. Sometimes kids do stupid things on repeat. It doesn't mean they're stupid people.

As for Marvin, he's still in New Orleans and we talk on the phone a couple of times a week. We always say, "Much love, my brother," before we hang up.

19

Linda Ronstadt

In 1984 the Neville Brothers were playing at Pete Fountain's club during the New Orleans World's Fair. Linda Ronstadt was there too, performing with Nelson Riddle and his orchestra at the Amphitheatre. After her show she came to hear us. Someone told me that she was in the audience, so I dedicated the song "Arianne" to her, then called her up onstage to sing with us. I didn't know her, but I knew of her. She'd come to a couple of our shows, so I just took a chance. She had told someone in the press that she doesn't do impromptu stuff like that, but she said she would never say no to Aaron Neville. We sang some doo-wop songs, like "You're Mine" and "We Belong Together" and "Earth Angel." The crowd loved it—and I did too.

I was hip to Linda from back when she sang "A Different Drum" with the Stone Poneys in the mid-'60s. I had heard "Desperado," too, which came out in 1973, and I was a big fan of her voice. That's what made it so special for her to come up onstage with us.

Later she told the press it was the highlight of her visit and that she felt like Cinderella at the ball because she got to sing with her favorite band and her favorite singer. And honestly, I felt like the handsome prince, having her sing with us. After the show I asked for her autograph and she wrote, "To Aaron, I'll sing with you any time, any place, anywhere, in any key."

So the next year Allen Toussaint and I invited her to come down and sing at the NOAHH benefit, and she said yes. We met at Sea-Saint Studio with Allen and Linda's manager, Peter Asher, to figure out what we would all be performing. When singers get together, we sing. It's pretty much always going to happen. Allen was sitting at the piano, and Linda and I realized we both knew "Ave Maria" because we'd learned it in Catholic school—"Ave Maria," that song that went through my bloodstream and was curing me when Joel left. Me and Linda started it in harmony, bringing it to another dimension. Our voices blended like pure silk. We were singing not just the notes but the world inside the notes. Everything has a purpose, a meaning, and when I sing that song, I want to cleanse the world. All of that was there when we sang it together.

Peter said, "*Wow!* You should do a record together."

I said, "No doubt," keeping it cool. In truth, I was geeked to be talking about recording with the great Linda Ronstadt.

It took until 1988 to make it happen, but it was well worth the wait. Linda was working on her album *Cry Like a Rainstorm, Howl Like the Wind*, and I ended up singing on four of the tracks. We recorded that album at Skywalker Ranch, George Lucas's studio (Linda was dating him at the time), which was pretty cool.

Being in the recording studio with Linda was magic. We respected each other's voices. She said that our voices are married and we probably sang together in another life. She's a small woman, but she has a really big voice. But when she sang with me, she pulled it back a little and came down to my sweet sound. It was like twins singing.

The song everyone remembers from that album is "Don't Know Much." Linda knew Cynthia Weil, one of the composers (Barry Mann and Tom Snow are the other two), and she picked it for the album.

When something really special happens, onstage or in a studio, the performers know it, even when there's no audience. Everybody who was there in the recording studio that day knew that song was a hit from the jump. When we got out of the studio afterward, I said to her, "Meet you at the Grammys." I was joking but not joking. For sure we'd done something special.

In the video for that song we put our arms around each other and looked into each other's eyes in a really deep way. Linda touched my face and lips kind of sexy, and we kissed at the end. It started all kinds of rumors about how there was something going on between Linda and me. Like we got married and she moved into my house and even that we were going to have a baby. But here's the truth. We made the video in New Orleans on St. Charles Avenue, right down the street from where Daniel Lanois recorded the Neville Brothers album *Yellow Moon* that same year. The director told us, "If you don't make it look real there ain't no sense in doing it." Well, it was easy to make it look real. I mean, Linda is a beautiful lady, so all we had to do was look into each other's eyes. Every man likes to look at a beautiful woman. But the deal was that we really respected each other and loved to sing together, and that's the whole thing. Joel was there when we made the video, and she knew that's all there was between us.

Linda is the sweetest person in the world. She's like the girl next door, plus an amazing singer. She could belt it out one minute and come to the angel part of her voice the next. I have mad respect for her.

"Don't Know Much" reached number two on the *Billboard* Hot 100 in the UK and number one on the *Billboard* Adult Contemporary chart. It was number one in Ireland and Canada, number two in Australia, and reached the top five in Austria, Belgium, the Netherlands, and New Zealand. It seemed like you were hearing it everywhere you went. *People* magazine wrote, "Their voices fuse like sunlight beaming through a stained-glass window." It was pretty crazy.

Linda called to tell me we'd be singing "Don't Know Much" at the 1990 Grammys. That night, my nerves were working overtime. The way the song was presented, Linda was already onstage and I was supposed to come out from behind a big purple curtain and join her. I peeked through the curtain and saw Meryl Streep out in the audience—it was packed with Hollywood royalty—and I knew I was standing in front of the world on that stage, when you added in all the people watching on TV.

Linda was standing there in a sweet black dress with a poufy purple skirt, and I came out in my tuxedo and walked across the stage to sing with the great Linda Ronstadt. I was so nervous I almost tripped over the mic cord. Then the song started, and I had to sing while I was walking (everybody does that in music videos, but we don't do it much when we're actually singing onstage). My nerves were frazzled, until I got there and looked into her eyes. She looked at me and smiled, and it all smoothed out for me. Linda turned once during our song to face the audience, but I just looked at her the whole time; I felt safe looking at her. We danced onstage during the guitar solo, like we did in the video, and she gave me a kiss at the end. We got a standing ovation. I felt like a little boy who just got his first bicycle.

When I went up to get my Grammy, I remembered something a recording engineer at Sea-Saint, Skip Goodwin, used to tell me, back when I was doing drugs and feeling like I might never be heard. He was watching me go through all sorts of changes with record companies, and he told me, "Aaron, remember, patience is a virtue." When me and Linda won the Grammy, I wanted to tell Skip I finally got it. I had also been thinking about a thing I heard James Cagney say at the end of the movie *White Heat*: "Made it, Maw, top of the world." But before I could say either of those things, Linda whispered in my ear, "Don't forget to thank Joel"—which I was gonna do anyway—and I forgot about Skip and Jimmy Cagney.

The Neville Brothers won a Grammy that year as well, for best pop instrumental performance for "Healing Chant," which Charlie blew the shit out of on the album *Yellow Moon*. We were all in awe during the recording session of that one. That song and what he did with his sax stood out by itself.

If you watch the video on YouTube of Linda and me singing at the Grammys, you'll see that they covered up the tattoo on my cheek with a lot of makeup. It wasn't my choice. I guess maybe they felt I looked too much like a thug. The next night Linda and I were on the *Tonight Show* with Johnny Carson. I was big-time nervous; it was my first time being on a show like that. Linda told me she was nervous too, but she didn't show it. When we sang, I stood on her right side and turned toward her, so my tattoo was away from the camera, and they somehow angled it so you couldn't see the tattoo when we were talking to Johnny either.

A couple of years later, when I sang a duet with Ernie on *Sesame Street* (he is not nearly as beautiful as Linda), they covered it up again. There must be people who have only seen me sing on TV and are surprised to read in this book that I have a tattoo on my left cheek. But it's been with me all my life and it's a part of me.

Like I said, I wasn't surprised when Linda and I won a Grammy. What I didn't expect is that another song we recorded on that album, "All My Life," won the Grammy again the next year. Because I didn't think we would win, I didn't go to the ceremony. I was in the grocery store and this guy came out and said to me, "Hey, man, you won again!"

And I said, "What you talking about?"

He said, "You and Linda won with 'All My Life.'"

I was as thrilled as I was surprised.

After the Grammys the Neville Brothers toured with Linda for a while. We performed all over the United States and in Europe in big cities like Amsterdam, Paris, Vienna, and Brussels. I remember in London we stayed in this beautiful old hotel called Claridge's that looked like a palace inside.

It was a different time entirely from those Larry Williams tours where we stayed in segregated guesthouses (not even hotels) and sometimes had to run out down the drainpipe because Larry didn't want to pay the bill. I don't know if I thought about it then, but now I look back and I know I've come a long, long ways.

That tour with Linda kicked open a lot of doors for us and got a lot of people to listen to our music. People sometimes said that Linda introduced me to the world, but she always said she was following me. We'd open for her, and her fans showed plenty of love for the Nevilles. No doubt it gave the Brothers new fans. During her set, she'd call me back out onstage to sing "Don't Know Much" and a couple of other songs from her album. It was really special. If I was nervous, all I had to do was look into her eyes and it ran away the jitters—we would melt into each other. We would dance together on the guitar solo, and she'd always end the song by giving me a kiss. It was like magic being on the stage with her.

I remember one time we were singing at an outdoor amphitheater when a bug went down her cleavage. She went ballistic and had to do this kind of funny dance, beating her chest like a crazy person, to get it out. Her band kept playing, and in case you're wondering, we sure did finish the song. We all had a laugh about it afterward.

When we were out touring, I would ride on her bus sometimes, and we would try out new songs. She would talk about her days with the Stone Poneys and the Eagles, and I would talk about my time when I was touring with "Tell It Like It Is." It was another era, and she was really interested in how it was for me back then, and how different it was from when she started touring.

We had so much love and respect for each other that our duets made love. And that brought people to believe we were more than singing partners. But we were just really great friends—me and Linda, and Joel too. Linda and I still talk all the time and I don't believe that we would be friends now if I had ever made a move on her.

In 1991 Linda said she'd like to produce a solo album with me, along with George Massenburg, the legendary recording engineer who'd worked with us on *Cry Like a Rainstorm*. He actually builds recording boards, and I have much respect for him. Another no-brainer, as far as I was concerned. It was my first solo album since the 1972 record I did with Allen Toussaint. It's called *Warm Your Heart*, and the album was filled with nothing but great songs, most of which Linda picked. She arranged for a lot of amazing musicians to play on that album, including Bob Seger on vocals and Russ Kunkel on percussion. I am still so proud of that record.

My friend from way back, Mac Rebennack (a.k.a. Dr. John), knew that I was a big Clyde McPhatter fan, so he recommended I sing an old Clyde chestnut, "Warm Your Heart." It's one of my all-time favorite songs. Mac played piano on it and took a killer solo. Mac and I had been friends since we were teenagers, and the first time I stepped into a recording studio was when I was about sixteen and he asked me to sing background on one of the records he was producing for his band, Roland Stone and the Skyliners. So we'd come a long ways.

Linda turned me on to two Allen Toussaint songs that I had never heard before: "That's the Way She Loves" and "With You in Mind." Then she picked a John Hiatt song called "Feels Like Rain," which really gave me a chance to showcase my vocal range. Ry Cooder played slide guitar on that song and on an old traditional spiritual called "I Bid You Good Night," where he had a magnificent solo that really blew me away.

And then we did "Louisiana 1927," written by Randy Newman. The song is about the Great Mississippi Flood of 1927, which left seven hundred thousand people homeless in Louisiana and Mississippi. (Years later, after Hurricane Katrina, I sang that song on TV for *A Concert for Hurricane Relief*.)

Rita Coolidge did a duet with me on "La Vie Dansante," a Jimmy Buffett song. And Linda and me did another duet, "Close Your Eyes," an old Chuck Willis song from the 1950s.

"Everybody Plays the Fool" was a hit in 1972 for the R&B group The Main Ingredient, but Russ Kunkel revised it so it sounded a little like reggae. (A lot of people don't know this, but Linda was the one whistling on that song.) "Angola Bound," a song about getting on that prison bus, my brother Charlie helped me write. Cyril played the congas on the track and my son Jason did the rap part, which was so cool. It was the first time I recorded with Jason. He had been a rapper/singer and break dancer for a few years already, so he was seasoned for it. (Eventually, he formed his own group, Jason Neville Funky Soul Band, with his wife, Lirette, and they gig all over New Orleans now and put on a great show.)

Linda reminded me how good she thought I sang "Ave Maria," so that was another no-brainer. But to take it to yet another level, she got me to blend with the boys choir from Grace Cathedral in San Francisco, and she sang the soprano part herself. We also recorded the Drifters song "Don't Go Please Stay," and the sound of the choir softened it up and made it something new. We recorded most of the record in Los Angeles, but for those two songs we actually recorded inside Grace Cathedral in San Francisco. The sound was so good in that cathedral, it was breathtaking. I felt like I was recording in heaven.

Warm Your Heart went platinum and "Everybody Plays the Fool" hit the Top 10 on the *Billboard* Hot 100 chart, reaching number eight in the fall and charting for twenty weeks. It got to number one on the *Billboard* Adult Contemporary chart and number two on the Hot R&B Singles. And it was a number one hit in New Zealand and charted really high in a lot of other countries. So me and the Brothers did another tour.

After getting the Grammys with Linda and the Neville Brothers, me and Joel were able to move out of our shotgun house on Valence Street and buy a house in New Orleans East, east of the Industrial Canal and north of the Mississippi River, a newer area that's a little bit like a suburb. Our Great Auntie Leelah gave that old house to me and my brother Artie; that's where we lived when Jason was born, and it gave us many years of comfort. It was a wholesome neighborhood back then, and just a few blocks from Tipitina's. But the neighborhood had changed and it had become a drug hotspot. Me and Joel were really glad to get the children up from there.

We kept the house, though. And unknown to me and Joel, Jason had unlocked a little side window and he and Aaron Jr. went back up there and were selling cocaine and some crack in the house. One night in 1992, me and Joel got a call from my friend Rooney's mom, Mrs. Louise, saying we better come uptown because the police had Aaron Jr. and Jason on the ground outside the house—a dreaded sight.

At that time crack had come out and it was like wildfire in the neighborhood. We were watching all the young kids getting caught up in it, and that's why we felt like we needed to get out of there. But Aaron and Jason were on it too, and selling a little was a way to get the money for their drugs. They weren't big-time dealers; it was just part of being in the game.

The charge was that they had sold a rock of crack to somebody. Jason took the rap from Aaron, and that started him on his trek of doing time. He was a little boy who got caught up in some grown-up things. Aaron sat in the parish prison a couple of months (his first and last time in jail), but the charge didn't stick because Jason took it all.

We had to talk to lawyers and go to court with him and watch him get sent up. They sentenced him to nine years in Angola. When they said nine years—all that time—my heart sank. It was devastating for me and Joel. Me being friends with Warden Cain, I knew the warden would look out for him. But I know how jail is, and him being a young boy, I was so worried.

I wouldn't say Jason was following in my footsteps; he was following his own footsteps. But it made me think about what me being in the game had done to my father. Poppee had certain expectations of me, and I guess I blew it—starting way back with that tattoo on my cheek. I was thinking about what me and Charles doing drugs did to him. He died young, at fifty years old. At least before he died I was able to buy him a car out of the money I got from Par Lo.

We kept fighting for Jason. Finally, a judge decided the sentence was too harsh, and he and the governor helped us get it reduced to two and a half—which is still hard time for a kid who's just twenty going in.

20

I Still Call Them Albums

I had to lie on the floor in the aisle between the seats on that long-ass flight home from New Zealand back in 1991. When I got home and went to the hospital, I found out that I had a bulging disk pressed up against a nerve that touched everything in my back. The first doctor said he wanted to operate. I said I wanted a second opinion. The next doctor told me operating was the last thing he wanted to do—he'd had his back operated on once, and when he woke up the next day, he thought he'd be able to do the same things he did before. But it didn't happen like that, and he was messed up for the rest of this life. He didn't want that for me.

He sent me to a stress relief chiropractor and started me on pain pills. I prayed a whole lot because I thought that pain would be there forever. Eventually it went away. But the pills—well, I had no problem getting them either from a doctor or on the street. They did not go away as quick as the pain did.

In October, while I was seeing the chiropractor, the great Bill Graham died. He was leaving a Huey Lewis concert at the Shoreline Amphitheater in San Francisco and his helicopter hit the power line. That Halloween the Neville Brothers did a show at the New Orleans Municipal Auditorium that we dedicated to Bill Graham. They had a chair set up for me that looked like a throne, and even though I was sitting down my voice was extra powerful. Once I started singing, the pain didn't mean nothing. I sang at a memorial concert for Bill the next week in San Francisco, too, in Golden Gate Park. I was sitting down singing "Ave Maria" while a ballerina danced.

Bill Graham kicked down a lot of doors and made a lot happen for us. He was like a ray of sunshine in what can be a very dark business. It was a very sad day when he was taken from us.

Morty Wiggins took up where Bill left off, and we kept touring. In 1992 we went to Modena in Italy to take part in a Pavarotti and Friends concert. The Brothers did a short set, and then I was supposed to sing "Ave Maria" with Pavarotti. But he was having problems with his throat, so he sat on the side of the stage and watched me with his hand on his jaw. When Pavarotti sings, he belts it out, but I was singing it so soft and sweet. When I was done he said to me, "Wow, how'd you do that?"

Around that time I had a solo concert in Hong Kong and Shanghai. The Hong Kong concert was shown on TV all over China, so I think about three hundred million people saw it. What I remember about Shanghai was all the people riding bicycles and wearing masks because of the pollution. I thought about how it might affect my asthma; I think that was the first time I was really aware of what all came along with touring.

Before that tour to Japan and New Zealand, I had a part in a movie called *Zandalee*, starring Nicolas Cage, Judge Reinhold, and Erika Anderson. It came out in 1991. I played a bartender at a bar at Rampart and Conti Streets in New Orleans. Nicolas was really funny in between takes. He would keep flubbing his lines and then turning to me and Judge and making faces. It cracked us up. And he kept doing it over and over. One thing about being in a movie or video is that you're always doing things over and over, so that after a while you're just glad when it's finished.

Actually, that wasn't my movie debut. I told you Artie introduced me to John Goodman. John and Dennis Quaid had done the movie *The Big Easy* together in 1986, so they were friends. (They used "Tell It Like It Is" in that movie—but when you get a song in a movie they just pick up your track and pay you some money; you don't actually have anything to do with the movie.)

Back then there was a little club called Benny's Bar on the corner, just steps away from our house on Valence Street. Cyril started up the music there, and any time John and Dennis came to New Orleans, they hung out at Benny's. I used to go there sometimes, although the truth is I could sit on my front porch and hear the music. (Actually, I could hear the bass and the drums coming up through the floor of my bedroom at three in the morning.)

We all hung out together, and I ended up playing a small part in the 1988 movie *Everybody's All-American* with John and Dennis,

Jessica Lange, and Timothy Hutton. I was Man with Gun. We did the shoot in Baton Rouge, because it was about Gavin Grey (a.k.a. the Grey Ghost), a football star at LSU. There was a foot race between the Grey Ghost and a Black guy named Blue, and my line was, "Blue gon' kick his ass." It was my first time acting, and it was way cool. I definitely wanted to do more.

Then in 1994 I was in *The Last Ride*, which starred Mickey Rourke as a rodeo rider and a bad character. We did a scene where he was in prison and I was his next-door cellmate, telling him that he ought to change his rowdy ways. Sitting around shooting the shit in jail is something I know something about, so it was easy for me. It was filmed at the Old Montana Territorial Prison in Deer Lodge, Montana, where they once kept Butch Cassidy and the Sundance Kid. Mickey stayed in character—kind of crazy and weird—the whole time we were filming, even between takes.

The Brothers kept recording: *Family Groove* in 1992, *Mitakuye Oyasin Oyasin* (which means "all my relations" in the Lakota language) in 1995, and *Valence Street* in 1999. Different producers had different ideas of what they thought we should sound like, and mostly they were more into what they wanted to hear than what we were actually doing. They're not bad albums, but the pure funk and fire isn't really there. *The Neville Brothers Live at Tipitina's* from back in 1982 was the funkiest band we ever had, and, in my opinion, that was some of the greatest music of all time. We were Mean Willie Green on drums, Daryl Johnson on bass and vocals, Brian Stoltz on guitar and vocals, and us four badass brothers. When I walk on my treadmill now, I listen to that album and I can walk, run, dance forever.

Meanwhile, I was busy with my own recordings. In 1993 I made an album called *The Grand Tour*, which was produced by Steve Lindsey for A&M. I made a deal with the record company that I would be able to do something spiritual on each record, since they weren't ready to do a whole spiritual record, so on that one I sang "The Lord's Prayer." Steve asked me to do the George Jones song "The Grand Tour," and I'm so glad he did. I got to meet George a bit later, and he said, "I've just gotta meet this young fellow who's singing my song better than me." George was one of the all-time greats, so that really gave me a laugh. I asked him why did they call him Possum, and he said, "Well heck, I look like a damn possum."

Steve used to have this singer named Warren Weibe demo songs for me that we were thinking about putting on the album. Warren had a great voice, and when Steve would send me the demo I'd think, "Warren's already done this song. There's not much more I can do with it." Warren did a lot of songs for David Foster, too, and recorded with Celine Dion and Gloria Estefan, but never really hit it big. He was an amazing vocalist, which just goes to show that some of what makes you successful is hard work and the right people, but some of it is luck, too.

Then later that year I did my Christmas album with producer Steve Lindsey, *Aaron Neville's Soulful Christmas*, which was a combination of spiritual songs and some funky ones.

The next year Tammy Wynette invited me to do a duet with her called "All I Am to You"—a deeply spiritual song. When we met up, she told me she loved my rendition of "The Grand Tour," especially the little curlicue I put on the last notes of George's song. I mean, I felt like I was in the studio with royalty, because, really, George was the king of country, and Tammy was the queen. "All I Am to You" was a great song, and it gave me and the Brothers a big following among the country music fans. It was on Tammy's last album, and I'm glad I got a chance to sing with her.

That year the legendary producer Don Was (who worked on the Rolling Stones' later albums) was putting together a record called *Rhythm Country and Blues*, with blues singers doing duets with country singers. He asked me and Trisha Yearwood to sing the old Patsy Cline song "I Fall to Pieces." We recorded it in New Orleans.

Trisha told me at the session that she used to listen to Linda Ronstadt when she was a little girl and try to copy her. And if I closed my eyes while she was singing that day, I could have thought it was Linda. We rehearsed and recorded the song—and made the video—all in less than a day. We were each in our own little recording booth and looked at each other through a glass window so we could follow each other word for word. We both came in ready— that's a respect thing—and we hit it dead on each time. We didn't do a lot of takes, and that's how it was with me always. Most of my solo albums I'd do different takes on a song and most of the time they'd end up using the first take, because it was the innocence— not thinking about the song and just singing it.

Don Was was kind of fawning all over us at the session, he was so happy. He had this thing where if he liked what you were doing, he'd pop his fingers on both hands. That means you know it was cool.

The session just felt on, and we all knew it was something special. As it turned out, we were not the only ones who thought so, because we won a Grammy in 1995. I didn't go to the Grammys that time, because by then I was tired of touring and when I was home I wanted to be home. I got invited to the Oscars a couple of times too, and I thought, for what? I'm not going to get an Oscar. Those shows are three hours long—who wants to sit there all that time? I watch those things on TV.

My next album (yes, I still call them albums) was *The Tattooed Heart*, produced by Steve Lindsey again, which came out in 1995. We did a promotional thing at a tattoo parlor in LA, so I let them go over the dagger on my cheek and freshen it up. The album had some great ballads on it, like "My Precious Star," "For the Good Times," and "Can't Stop My Heart from Loving You" (which was a hit for me), and also some of that doo-wop I love, like "Crying in the Chapel."

That year I got to meet another one of my idols, Curtis Mayfield. I loved him when he was with the Impressions back in the '60s, and when he went solo he brought some sharp (and no doubt well-deserved) criticism to what was going on in America at that time. Curtis was paralyzed from his neck down in 1990 when a lighting fixture fell on him onstage during an outdoor concert in Brooklyn, and while he couldn't play the guitar no more, he kept singing. I was appearing at a benefit concert for the Rhythm and Blues Founda-tion, which Bonnie Raitt founded in 1987 to assist R&B artists who needed help, and she arranged for me to spend two hours with Cur-tis. I sat next to him and would sing one of his songs and make him smile, and then he was talking to his people telling them what he wanted them to do, like he wasn't paralyzed, just handling his busi-ness. I had even more love and respect for this great pioneer.

On that same trip I saw my old friend Billy Guy from the Coast-ers. I didn't recognize him—he wasn't looking like he used to look—but I recognized his voice when he called me *Aaaaaaron*. I said, "Billy Guy, I'd know that voice anywhere." At that same event I hung out with the Ice Man (a.k.a. Jerry Butler), Ben E. King, and another of my heroes, Pookie Hudson of the Spaniels. Hanging out with all that serious talent, I felt like I belonged.

And then, in 1996, me and Linda got invited to sing at the White House for President Bill Clinton. It was all arranged through Linda's people, and was one of the In Performance at the White House concerts that were shown on public television. I just showed up in a white suit (not my favorite thing to wear onstage). Getting into the White House was not as weird as I thought it would be. They had Secret Service everywhere, but everything was arranged and it was pretty easy.

The concert was in a big tent outside, and Linda started off with a mariachi band and did her songs. Then she called me up. She said, "The last time I played in a tent, it was at the New Orleans Jazz and Heritage Festival," and everybody started applauding, and then she called me up to sing with her. She said, "Aaron sings like an angel; he is an angel; no, he's an archangel."

I'd actually met Clinton a couple of times before when he was trying to get elected and Linda and I sang at some fundraisers. So when I was onstage I said that I'd shook his hand and he felt human. I remember he applauded at that.

My last album on A&M was 1997's *To Make Me Who I Am*. Mark Mazzetti was the producer. I had the luxury of singing with

Linda again, on "Please Remember Me." I also had the great joy of being able to finally record the song I made from the poem I had to stand up in front of my sixth-grade class and recite, "Lovely Lady Dressed in Blue," which I put to music that dark night in New York before recording the Neville Brothers album *Fiyo on the Bayou* and then going into rehab. The title song came about when I was talking with the coproducer Robbie Nevil (not a relative of ours; a brother from another mother). I was telling him a part of my life story, and he looked at me and said, "Now that sounds like a song." So I wrote it that night and we recorded it the next day. It was easy looking back over my life that way; it was like a testimony. That's my son Ivan on the piano, by the way.

In 2003 Ivan got together a monster funk band called Dumpstaphunk for a one-off gig at the Jazz Fest. The band proved so badass that they stayed together, and now it's got his cousin Ian Neville on guitar, Nick Daniels and Tony Hall on bass, and drummer Deven Trusclair. Ivan's having a long musical career, and he made some great albums solo and with Dumpstaphunk. But I think just like with the Neville Brothers, the record companies don't always know how to market him.

Next I was able to do two gospel albums: *Devotion* in 2000 and *Believe* in 2003. I'd formed my own record label by then, Tell It Records, so I could record what I wanted to. Those records, which I love, was my giving back to God for all the favors He did for me. I knew the record company wasn't ready for albums like that, so I produced them myself. And between recording the two of them, I finally got tired of all the opiates I was taking. My back was feeling okay and I wanted to get off those pills. Ivan told me that he'd read about how people who tried to kick cold from pills could have a stroke or something else serious. So I decided to go to rehab again.

Ivan had had a stay at Las Encinas, a recovery center in Pasadena, and he hooked me up with them. They were close by Mount Wilson, where I did my time fighting forest fires. Dr. Drew Pinsky, who I guess is famous now, was the director. I remember we were talking about the pills I was taking, and he said, "One's too many and a thousand's not enough." It made all the sense in the world.

I went up there for a month, then stayed an extra week to be sure. I came home to Eastover, in East New Orleans, where me and Joel had moved back in 1991.

What can I say about Ivan and me going to the same rehab? My devil was heroin and his was crack cocaine. He moved to LA in 1981 and that made it even more accessible to him. I tried to give advice, when he and his brothers would listen, but I knew from experience that he had to figure it out for himself. At one time Fred and Jason wound up in LA with Ivan, and they would call me once or twice a week asking me to Western Union them money for this and for that. I knew what they were doing, and I'm glad we all made it to the other side of it.

After rehab I felt a lot better, but in 2002 my asthma, which I had sort of outgrown, came back on me with a vengeance. While I was out on the road with the Brothers, I would end up in the ER in places like Wichita and Austin and Albuquerque. If we were in a small club, the smoke from the audience would set it off. But the cedar trees or dust in the air could send me to the hospital too.

The next year, I made an album of standards, *Nature Boy*, for Verve. It was produced by Rob Mounsey, who wrote the most badass beautiful charts, and featured some hard hitters at the bat: Rob on piano, the incredible Ron Carter on bass, Grady Tate on drums, Roy Hargrove on trumpet, Anthony Wilson on guitar, and Ray Anderson on trombone. I flew to New York to do the session and was staying at the Meridian Hotel. When I got on the elevator and pushed the button, I must've picked up something from it, because when I got to my room I started coughing uncontrollably, like every six seconds. So I had to put the session on hold and fly back to New Orleans until I got over whatever it was. We recorded a month later, and it was a thrill to be there with all of those hard hitters. My brother Charlie, the horn man, played sax on "Since I Fell for You," and Linda Ronstadt sang with me on "The Very Thought of You." I dedicated the album to Uncle Jolly and my father, whom I saw as definitely nature boys the way they were traveling all over the world on ships.

Early in 2004 the Neville Brothers made what would be our last album together. It's called *Walking in the Shadow of Life* and it was a family affair. Ivan coproduced it and played piano, and Artie's son Ian played the guitar. Aaron Jr. and Cyril's son, Omari, played the drums and sang. We did a great remake of the 1970 Temptations song "Ball of Confusion," and one I wrote called "Junkie Child"—a subject I knew a lot about. There was also a great song called "Fallen Soldiers" that Ivan, Aaron Jr., and Jason wrote together. It was so cool to sing it with them.

The Neville Brothers kept touring through 2012. When we had new records out, the touring was continuous, sometimes six months a year, sometimes more. That's why I tried to take Joel out with me and not just leave her at home. We were also making solo albums and group albums and working on our own projects when we weren't touring. Artie'd had his back operated on twice and all that travel was hard on him. After almost forty years on the road, I guess we were all tired.

We had been closing out Jazz Fest, the position of the most honor, for more than twenty years. But in 2013 Art, Cyril, and Charles performed during the first weekend under a new name, The Nevilles. I closed it with my new band, then handed the torch to Trombone Shorty (a.k.a. Troy Andrews).

Our last gig was in our hometown, New Orleans, in 2015, and it was bittersweet. It was a sold-out gig at the Saenger Theatre. Keith Richards, who'd played with Artie and Cyril and the Meters, came down to New Orleans to play with us at that show. I looked at my brothers with love for our lives on the road. Sometimes I would be listening to them onstage and get so caught up in what they were laying down that I'd forget when it was my time to come in. I was always among royalty, no doubt. We all knew we were at the end of that road, but it still wasn't easy.

I remember so many times when me and my brothers went to foreign lands, and the people didn't speak English but understood our hearts from the vibrations of our voices. They showed us love, and we accepted it by showing it back to them. It was such a sincere welcoming from our families across the seas, our sisters and brothers from different mothers. I have friends all over the world now. I'll always love y'all till my time to leave. God bless us one and all.

21

We Laid Joel to Rest

In 2004 Joel had this cough that wouldn't go away. A friend of ours who lived next door, Chris Bloom, was a doctor, so I asked him to come over and look at her. He said she should have a CAT scan. She did, and they found a spot on her lungs. The doctors tested a piece and said it was really bad small cell lung cancer, close to her trachea, which made it inoperable. Joel's brother Vincent was a surgeon, and he looked at the scan and agreed.

Her cancer doctor gave her three months to live, and she said to him, "In other words, you're giving me a death sentence." When Joel said that, it hit me in the heart. I felt like it was a death sentence for me too.

But Joel was the toughest woman I ever met, and she was not the kind to lie down and die. The two of us, along with my sister Athelgra, started crawling up the stairs on our knees at the St. Ann's

Shrine and praying at the St. Jude Shrine every day. Joel took her chemotherapy and didn't let anything stop her. I would take her to the cancer center and sit with her while she got the chemo. I watched her lose her beautiful hair. She put on a wig and kept going. She was a strong little woman.

Three months came and went. After a while, she seemed to be getting a little better. I went back out on the road.

Then in August 2005 we all heard on the news that a huge hurricane was heading for New Orleans. City officials said Eastover, where we lived, was in the safe zone. But back in 1965 when Hurricane Betsy hit, the levees broke, flooding the Ninth Ward where a lot of Black people own homes. People said the levees were dynamited back then to protect the French Quarter, although it was never proved one way or the other. I wasn't taking any chances.

I told everyone to meet me where I was, in Memphis. Joel, her family, our kids and their families, my sister and her husband all packed up three days' worth of clothes, thinking we'd be back home soon. Artie and his family, who lived Uptown, were the only ones who stayed behind. We all sat in a motel in Memphis and watched on TV as Hurricane Katrina slammed into New Orleans.

And then the levees broke—again. People said afterward that they heard explosions just before it happened, and it was suspect, for sure. On TV we saw the water coming. Everyone was glued to the TV and saw the same thing at the same time and knew the truth that we weren't going back home.

The authorities told us our house was in the safest part of New Orleans, but they were wrong. There were bodies floating in the water all through Eastover. Plus there were alligators and snakes and all kinds of things swimming around. And all the toxic chemicals. Back when I used to work on the docks, I'd see the rail cars full of nasty-smelling stuff that would fizz or smoke when it rained, so I knew what was in that floodwater. Sometimes when the wind blows a certain way in Eastover, people still get sick.

Our house had ten feet of water in it for a couple of days. That water was filled with chemicals and dead things and anything else you could think of. When the water finally went down, Joel paid someone to go over there and take whatever could be saved. They sent us some photos, and we could see that everything was busted up. A great big refrigerator was thrown on its back. My baby grand piano was flattened into a pile of wood and wire. I was hoping to get back some of my photos and records and tapes, but the mold and mildew had already started growing, and whatever was in the house was ruined—including a painting I really loved that Peter Max did of me, and a photo of me and Ben E. King, Jerry Butler, and Pookie Hudson that I cherished. And all my other photos, posters from my shows, the pair of wrestling boots that Bret "the Hitman" Hart gave me and the boxing gloves from Mickey Rourke—gone like the pictures I left on the subway in New York a long time ago.

I felt violated. I never went back to that house.

We lost a lot of music, but many of our tapes were with our friend John Brenes out in Oregon. He used to come to our shows a lot, and we let him tape them, including the duo concerts I'd done in Club Lingerie in Los Angeles and in Brooklyn and New Orleans with Amasa Miller—just private stuff. I am so thankful to John that he saved the tapes.

There was no water in Art's house, thank God, but New Orleans, my home that I thought would be there forever, was devastated. Some people lost everything and didn't have the means to get it back. We were lucky enough to have insurance and were eventually able to sell the house, but I didn't want anything out of it. While we only lost material stuff, a lot of people had lost their lives. I was bitter. I was mad, too.

For the Nevilles, every neighborhood in the city was our neighborhood. Our neighbors were hurting; we were all hurting. To help in the best way we could, we sang at a lot of benefit concerts, including From the Big Apple to the Big Easy, and went on a lot of TV shows, like *Larry King* and *Jay Leno*, to encourage people to help. They would always want me to sing the song "Louisiana 1927" by Randy Newman. It was really emotional for me to sing that song; sometimes I could barely get it out.

Joel and me did not go back to New Orleans. Our attorney, Craig Hayes, and his wife, Pam, were living in Nashville at the time, so the family moved to a hotel there and they helped us find a house to rent in nearby Brentwood. A friend of ours, Tom Morgan from North Carolina, helped us and many more folk by giving us and everyone in New Orleans great mattresses and sheets and pillows. Our neighbors Ron and Stacy Turk helped our grandkids get into the local school and gave us some household stuff we might need. And their kids, Natalie and Austin, befriended my grandkids and helped them feel at home. You manage to find good people everywhere. When you look for them, there's always some.

Joel's mother, Beatrice, her sister, Betinna, and her brother John, who had lost their own homes in Pontchartrain Park, stayed with us, and my sister and her husband, Earnest, came up too. Joel's hospital in New Orleans was gone, but we found some good doctors at Vanderbilt Hospital who helped her keep living and fighting the cancer.

So we were all together when her cancer came back on in the spring of 2006. It had invaded her bones and her brain. She did the chemo and radiation like a champ, and I'd sit with her and hold her hand. She insisted on showing everyone how tough she was; like she would tell the people at the cancer center that she didn't need a wheelchair to leave the place, and she'd walk out leaning on my arm. I have never met anyone stronger in my life.

That year I recorded *Bring It on Home . . . The Soul Classics*, mostly at a studio nearby in Franklin, Tennessee. All those great songs, like "Ain't No Sunshine When She's Gone" and "Stand by Me," suddenly turned into prayers. I didn't want to lose her. The week before Christmas I was performing with my quintet in Nashville, singing the Jimmie Rodgers song "Why Should I Be Lonely," and I just broke down. I got halfway through and couldn't sing anymore.

We all gathered at our house for New Year's Eve—and to say goodbye. Joel took it for as long as she could, a few days more, but her last night, about eleven p.m., she said, "Jesus, what's taking you so long?" I held her small hands in my big ones, and I knew she was hurting so bad, but I couldn't help her. At two a.m. on January 5, 2007, as she lay with her family all around her, Jesus finally came for her.

I'm not sure what I felt at that moment. I was just unexplainably numb.

Joel had bought a mausoleum at Mount Olivet Cemetery on Gentilly Boulevard, and made it very clear that's where she wanted to be laid to rest. So the next day Athelgra and our daughter Ernestine went back to New Orleans to make arrangements.

Suddenly I was alone in our bedroom, and I started crying uncontrollably. I felt lost, like a duck out of water. Joel was the one who raised me after taking me from my mother's arms when I was just sixteen. She taught me and she guided me. I remember times I would be getting ready to go outside and Joel would say, "Aaron, where you going with that crazy-looking shit on?" and I would come back in and change. To her I was just Aaron, not a singing star.

She was definitely the boss in our family. She would dole out all the discipline, including the spankings. Our kids knew I was a teddy bear compared to Joel. Joel also took care of all our business. I didn't even know how to write a check.

She always spoke her mind, so if you didn't want to hear the truth then don't ask Joel, 'cause she definitely told it like it was. And even now, whenever we get together me and our kids laugh about her potty mouth. If someone was doing some dumb shit, her pet phrase was, "You simple-minded motherfucker." She used to text it to the kids in a kind of code: SMMF.

Joel was sixty-six when she died. She was about four and a half feet tall, but she was a giant. No one messed with her. She got plenty of respect, for sure.

Even when I was with Cyril and Charles up in New York, practically lost to the world, Joel kept me safe. Just thinking about her would stop me from doing the worst stuff. Hoping I could get back with her is what gave me a purpose. Now I had no purpose at all. I felt like I was losing my mind.

Joel hadn't taken a lot of the pain medicine they gave her, because she felt like it just made her crazy. So I stashed it away—morphine, Dilaudid, Percodan, Percocet. Meanwhile, the doctor had put me on some kind of pills for my nerves, but every time I laid down at night and tried to sleep, it felt like there were little creatures scurrying across the bed. So I stopped taking them. I thought, "I can't take this. I think Joel's got something better." And she did.

Five days later, on January 10, I flew back to New Orleans with Joel's mother and her brother John. Taking her home the last time was the hardest thing I ever had to do. I remember during the flight I buried my face in a book of sudoku, trying to point my mind anyplace except where it was pointing. Athelgra picked us up at the airport and dropped us off at a hotel downtown. It was the first time I'd been back since Katrina, and thinking about all those bodies and the poison in the water, I didn't even want to walk around. My asthma was pretty bad around then, and I wasn't taking any chances.

John and I went to Meyer the Hatter on St. Charles Avenue, where my dad and Uncle Jolly used to shop, and bought a couple of hats, and then I went back to the hotel.

Joel loved Our Lady Star of the Sea, a big Catholic church in the Eighth Ward where we knew the priest, Tony Ricard. In 2001 a New Orleans artist named Vernon Dobard painted a huge, heavenly scene called "The Dance of Holy Innocence" on the sanctuary wall. It shows eight beautiful angels of all races dancing around the Blessed Virgin Mary. Joel was laid out in an open coffin beneath the angels, wearing a black outfit with leopard-print trim. She looked like she was asleep in her coffin, like she'd never been sick. I said to her, "I know you're going to heaven, because I watched you go through hell. You were so strong. I just wish I could have your strength when my time comes."

At the memorial service, I remember Philip Manuel, our old friend from Valance Street, sang "Come Ye Disconsolate," Jason played a piano piece he wrote for his mom called "An Angel," and my brother Charles brought us all deep into his heart with a solo on his horn.

Then Cyril read something I'd written. He said for me, "I remember our first kiss back in 1957, and I'll never forget our last kiss. I held her head in my hands and was as gentle as I could be. I kissed her eyes, her face, and her hands. I knew I was losing my best friend. She was everything a person could be to another. I still feel her lips on mine. I'll never get over losing her. But I know she's in a better place. She's gone home."

Cyril was all choked up. He used to call Joel his second mother, and he'd try out new songs for her and greatly valued her opinion. He could barely finish reading what I wrote.

I didn't think I'd be able to say anything, but finally I found a little bit of my voice. I stood up in the front of the church and talked about how Joel and I met and got married. Then I said, "It's going to be the hardest thing in the world for me to accept that Joel is not there no more."

The next morning, Father Ricard said Joel's funeral mass. The church was packed, and even more friends sent flowers, including Linda Ronstadt, Trisha Yearwood, Garth Brooks, and John Goodman. The funeral home actually had to send a second car just to take all the flowers to the cemetery. Artie played the piano, then his daughter Arthel read a poem I wrote called "To My Lil Joel from Your Big Aaron." It said, "Through it all I've never seen anyone as strong and faithful as you. If I can be half that strong, I'll be all right."

There was more music, some speeches—honestly, I don't remember it all. We all marched out while the Rebirth Brass Band played "Just a Closer Walk with Thee." Then we got into cars and headed out to Mount Olivet Cemetery. Athelgra carved the names of Joel's family into her casket—a family tradition our Auntie Cat started because she was afraid someone might dig up her coffin and use it again.

And so we laid Joel to rest on our forty-eighth wedding anniversary.

22

Sarah

Either God or Joel or both sent Sarah Ann Friedman into my life to stop me from the downward spiral I was on. I truly believe it.

Joel's family, who were still living with me after Katrina, came home with me to Brentwood after her funeral. After all the objections they'd had to her and me getting together, her mother told me she was glad that I married her daughter. It felt good to hear that, but really, nothing felt good enough to break through the pain I was in. I'd taken what felt like a one-two-three punch of losing Joel, losing my house, and losing New Orleans. I was in deep.

All of Joel's pain pills were there in the house. Her doctors had given her all the good stuff—and by that I mean all the bad stuff. I started taking them for relief, even though they didn't give me any relief. After I ran out of Joel's meds, I got doctors to write me prescriptions for them, or I knew where to get them on the street. I was taking ten to fifteen pills a day. My family had no idea.

And I had to go back out on the road, because contracts had been signed, plus I was supporting a lot of people in that big house in Brentwood. Sometimes I'd feel the pressure when I wasn't doing good and still had to go out, so I went to a comfort zone that was familiar to me, which was getting high. I put on a lot of weight—I was up to two hundred and fifty pounds—and nothing (and by that I mean nobody) was stopping me.

Nobody knew what I was going through. I cried 24/7, and people would come and tell me, "I know what you're going through." I'd think, "You don't know what I'm going through." I didn't think it was possible for me to be happy again. But I didn't talk about it. I just swallowed it all along with the pills.

By early 2008 things were slowly getting back to normal in New Orleans, and Joel's family and most of mine were moving back. I was ready to leave Brentwood and be closer to New Orleans—just not in New Orleans. After Katrina I was hurricane-shy. I couldn't handle them anymore. We'd already run from quite a few. New Orleans is right in hurricane alley and is like a big bowl surrounded by water. Cyril used to say that we were really a tropical island that was hooked onto the USA. The levees around New Orleans are supposed to be what holds all that water back. But we'd all learned the hard way that they were not maintained and could break—or be broken—when things got bad enough.

So my business manager found me a house in Covington, Louisiana, right across Lake Pontchartrain and not far from Abita

Springs, where I'd gotten caught with a stolen car those many years ago. She had it renovated, and kind of went overboard, but it was a nice house and I learned to like it. I could sit outside and watch the sun go down, then drive on into New Orleans in about seventy minutes, straight along the causeway that ran across the lake.

In May 2008 me and the Brothers went back to New Orleans to do the first Jazz Fest after Katrina. Being at Jazz Fest felt good, but being in New Orleans again didn't. It's always been my heart, and my family is there, but to me New Orleans was Joel and Joel was gone. So I was thinking I'd get out of town as soon as we were finished.

People magazine wanted to do a profile of us, so they sent Sarah Friedman, a well-known photographer, to shoot the Neville Brothers. We met up at our office on Canal Street and took the pictures out on the balcony. Straight off, I was impressed by Sarah's strength and tenacity, as well as her talent and intelligence. She was so efficient and got everything done quick and perfect.

Sarah was also so pretty she took my breath away. I was smitten right then and there. It's hard to say exactly what it was, but she hypnotized me. Maybe it was her smile, her demeanor. Maybe it was her eyes—a shade of blue-gray that's almost impossible to describe. The whole session I was looking at her while she was taking the photos. She had an aura around her. I felt a tingle in my heart. I can't explain.

After the photo shoot, I stuck around the office to talk to her while she and her assistant were packing up their gear. Sarah had been to New Orleans a couple of times, including a shoot she did of the artists at Cash Money Records, a New Orleans hip-hop label that had Drake, Nicki Minaj, Lil Wayne, and a bunch of other big-timers. But she wasn't hip to the Neville Brothers, so we talked about music, I played a few songs for her, and I gave her a copy of *The Brothers*, a book the four of us wrote with the music journalist David Ritz back in 2001. I told her I wanted a book report, and we both laughed. Then I asked for her phone number, and she gave me her office number. It was a start.

I was determined to follow up, so maybe a couple of weeks later I called her and said, "Hi, this is Aaron Neville, and I want that book report now." She laughed and we talked and talked. I started calling her every few days, and I was excited like a kid every time I called. Her voice just went through my bloodstream. I didn't want to overdo it, so I always let a few days go by between calls. We could talk for hours, though, about what I did, what she does, some of the people she'd taken pictures of. After not too long I started feeling comfortable calling every day. Sarah listened to me talk about Joel, because it was heavy on me. I'd cry and it was a healing thing.

I went up to visit her in New York and we went out to dinner. She came down to see me in Covington. Pretty soon we were going back and forth a lot. I would pick her up at the airport, and when I saw her coming toward me there it went again, my heart doing flip-flops. I would take her hand and proudly walk her from the baggage area to my car. I felt so alive. When I'd bring her back to the airport and kiss her goodbye, right away I couldn't wait to see her again or just hear her voice over the phone.

Sarah used to come out on some of my gigs, and I went on some of hers. She had almost as much gear as the Neville Brothers' whole band, and she'd be handling a lot of it herself. I was really impressed. And it was exciting to look at her photos, to see all the people she had photographed. Sarah specialized in strong figures, like rappers, sports stars, Fortune 500 executives, hedge fund managers, and politicians. She sometimes had a very small window of time to get the shot, and she got it every time. She photographed all the rappers in New Orleans and everyone from Kanye West to LeBron James to Serena and Venus Williams to Barack Obama. Sarah is gangster, no doubt.

She is a strong, strong woman, and in that way, Sarah is like Joel. Some men are afraid of women with that deep inner strength, but for me, those are the women I love.

When I saw her it made me swoon, and when I kissed her it was like magic. I thought I would never be able to love again after Joel, but I was wrong. When I met Sarah, I didn't know how old she was and she didn't know how old I was. We fell in love and it didn't matter. I know for sure she saved my life in all kinds of ways. I was on a dangerous road, swallowing those pills like Scooby snacks, so I know I would have been either dead or close to it a long time ago.

One day we were down in Covington, getting ready to go out to eat, and I stuck my hand in my pocket to get my car keys. When I pulled it out, about fifteen Vicodins fell out onto the floor. Sarah was street smart and knew exactly what they were. I'll never forget the look she gave me. Then she said, "Oh no, I'm not going through this shit again." She had dated some guys who were junkies, and she'd had enough of that. She gave me a straight choice, and it was a no-brainer. I chose Sarah. I gave her all of the two hundred pills I had and she got rid of them. That was my last run with dope of any kind.

After that, we started talking about moving in together. So I went to New York in 2009 to be with her, and she helped me sell the house in Covington. I moved into her little apartment, a walk-up where she was hauling up hundreds of pounds of camera equipment. It was about time for her to move anyway, so we rented a place on Twenty-Third Street and Lexington Avenue.

People always ask me how it was to move from the Big Easy to the Big Apple. The truth is that I loved it. You feel like the apartment ain't that huge, but you own the whole city. I was in a New York state of mind.

That was the first time I went to a play on Broadway. We went to see *Fela!* about the Nigerian singer Fela Kuti. It just blew me away. We went to see a groovy Motown review and went backstage to meet the cast afterward. This kind of stuff was all new to me, and I enjoyed it to the utmost.

The last time I'd lived in New York was in the 1970s, and it was a whole other animal in those days. Even if I hadn't been living the junkie life back then, New York was a crazy place. But everything had changed. We'd go out walking at night, me and my beautiful Sarah Ann, and I always felt safe. Or we'd sit in the park together holding hands and I'd feel like a teenager. People knew who I was, and sometimes someone would ask for an autograph but in a very low-key way. A lot of times someone would just holler, "Legend!" or yell, "OG!" New York is full of celebrities, and New Yorkers know how to be cool about it.

There were so many great restaurants, and we had fun walking to them. If it was too far, we'd catch a taxi. Back in the '70s they wouldn't stop to pick me up, but it was a different scene now; they would pull up alongside and ask, "You want a cab?"

I was a New York musician now, and I sang at Lincoln Center with Wynton Marsalis and Paul Simon. I sang at Carnegie Hall a few times, too, including once with a New Orleans review that included the trumpet player Irvin Mayfield, and again at a Rock for the Rainforest concert with Sting, Pavarotti, Branford Marsalis, Elton John, and some other heavy hitters.

One day I was just walking down Fifth Avenue and I ran into Steve Jordan, the drummer for Keith Richards's band, X-Pensive Winos. Steve said, "Hey, Aaron, it's ironic that I walked up on you. Keith is doing a recording and there's a part that only you could add to it." So I went to the studio and laid down some high notes in the right places on a song called "Nothing on Me," from Keith's album *Crosseyed Heart*. Crazy shit like that could happen in New York.

Me and Sarah started traveling together, too, and I think this was my first time traveling where I wasn't also working. We went to Jamaica and to Turks and Caicos, which turned out to be our favorite spot. The water was a blue-green that was so clear you could look down and see your feet. We rented an apartment near the beach and fixed our own food. Some days we'd just lie on the beach and do blessed nothing.

Back home, we ended up getting two calico kittens who we named Turks and Caicos. They were jumping and running all over everything, and would get into squabbles that were always so cute. Turks likes to lie on my chest and look deep into my eyes, like she knows me. Sometimes I'll be looking at her and just ask, "Who are you?"

Sarah belonged to a gym, and we started working out together. I'd been working out since I'd done time in California, and I'd had trainers who pushed me when I needed it, like Tazzie Colomb in New Orleans and Jack Weed in Brentwood. And I needed a push now. So I started with Sarah as my trainer and eventually ended up with a badass guy named Andrie (a.k.a. Drago). I lost all my excess weight and got fit again.

Sarah knew I'd been a heroin addict, so she pushed me to get tested for hep C and AIDS. The doctor told me that I had gotten out of the game just in time to miss the AIDS epidemic. We didn't think nothing of sharing another guy's works, and that's a big way AIDS (and hep C too) made the rounds. Charlie said he heard our old running buddies Susu and Canty had died. He asked, "They OD?" No, it was AIDS.

Sometimes I look at my veins in my arm, knowing that God put them in me to circulate my blood through my body, and wonder how I ever stuck a needle in them so many times that now it's hard for a doctor or nurse to locate them to take my blood. I know I couldn't even think about misusing my body like that again. I ask God for forgiveness for misusing my precious body, my temple.

I'd had a colonoscopy at Vanderbilt Hospital before I left Brentwood and got a clean bill of health; the doctor told me I didn't have to have another one for five years. But Sarah talked me into doing it again anyway, and the doctor found polyps that would've turned cancerous if he hadn't got them out. So Sarah saved my life again.

She got me to go to a cardiologist, too, because sometimes my heart would race and I didn't know what was happening. The doctor told me I have atrial fibrillation, which is when your heart beats too fast or too slow or too irregular. It increases your risk of having a stroke. I think I had it for a while, and I do believe I would've been either dead or close to it if I hadn't got it treated. So thank you, Sarah, my earth angel; that's one more time you saved my life.

I flew out to Cleveland to meet Sarah's family, and it went a lot better than when I met Joel's family. Sarah's mother, Anita, her brother Eric, and her sisters, Rachel and Jessica, they accepted me into their family and really made me feel welcome. Her father, Ernie, was a psychiatrist, and was bedridden by the time I met him. We spent a lot of time talking, and I finally told him that I wanted to marry his daughter and was going to take good care of Sarah Ann. He was pleased. I'm so glad I got to hang out with him before he died.

We got married on November 12, 2010, at a fancy restaurant called 11 Madison Park in one of those old New York art deco skyscrapers downtown. My friend Father Tony Ricard from Our Lady Star of the Sea Church, the same priest who buried Joel, came up to marry us. Our wedding was not too big. Sarah's mother, Anita, came, and my sister and her husband, and some of our New York friends.

Even before we got married we were thinking about buying an apartment, so in 2009 Sarah did a credit check to find out how much of a mortgage we could get. I thought my credit was good, but I found out things had not been taken care of and my credit was in the toilet. Sarah started looking at my bank statements and credit cards, and it looked like a hornet's nest. She found money was being taken from me in all sorts of ways. She kept saying, "I hope I'm wrong about this." But she wasn't wrong. Some rotten stuff in Denmark, as they say.

Joel had always taken care of our personal family finances, and my business manager had been taking care of my business finances since way back when the Brothers first got together. When Joel got sick, my business manager stepped up (or so I thought) to handle everything. But actually she was taking care of herself—as in, helping herself to my money. I was being ripped off big time.

Music is a business, but I am not a businessman. It's hard enough being an artist; that's why artists hire managers. But then you have to trust these people to do you right. I wouldn't cheat anybody, so I figured everybody is like me. I guess I had been complacent. I guess I just trusted too much.

My credit was a mess, and I was in debt. My business manager had probably been cheating me since Joel got sick. Nobody knew until Sarah uncovered it. Of course this person denied everything, so we had to get a lawyer and sue for answers.

The business manager tried to save herself by pointing everyone in the opposite direction—toward Sarah. She implied Sarah was trying to get my money. Friends, and even family members, started saying maybe we should investigate Sarah. But I said, "No, Sarah has her own money. She's the one who found all this stuff. It's the business manager who has to be investigated." And that's what happened.

It ended up being an ugly court battle that dragged on for three years. There was a lot of pointing fingers and lying and nastiness that went along with the deep investigating. It took its toll on us, but mostly on Sarah, who neglected her photography career to help me get my life straightened out. It was really rough for her.

In the end, the court found that I'd been cheated big time. We finally made a settlement with the business manager that included some compensation, but it was a fraction of what she'd stolen from me. I lost a lot of money, but you can't get back what isn't there anymore. Sarah and me were both pissed.

When all this was finally settled, we were able to buy our apartment. We got a good deal on a place on Ninth Street and Broadway, right on the dividing line between the East Village and the West Village. We were up on the fourteenth floor and had a beautiful little terrace. Sarah had a screened-in cat terrace built out there for Turks and Caicos, because we wouldn't trust them not to go leaping over the railing after a bird.

She also started planting things in big pots on the terrace, like tomatoes, cucumbers, shisito peppers, watermelon, strawberries, and even corn. She made friends with a farmer named Trina at the Union Square Farmers Market and a guy who sold plants there, and both of them gave her great information about how to grow things. Sarah took it all in and got to be a terrace farmer—which is a New York thing, I guess. She had a green thumb, and she was just as gung-ho about growing things as she was with her camera.

We put a string of lights across the terrace and would sit out there at night and stargaze or moongaze. We started calling our little terrace Chez Freville—a mash-up of our last names.

When I looked into Sarah's eyes, my heart was stolen. We connected so deeply. It was like I was a chrysalis being born again as a butterfly. It's hard to explain, but being with her made my senses way keen; I could see things so clearly. Every day was brand new, refreshing. I looked forward to just walking the streets of Manhattan with Sarah. My life had been renewed.

The next year, 2012, I got to do something I'd been dreaming about. For years I'd watched nature shows on TV with the lions and wildebeests in Africa, and I wanted to see it for myself. So Sarah and I went on a safari.

We stayed at these places that were like permanent tents with a valet who would bring us breakfast and coffee and juice in the morning, and would put special foot warmers in the bed to keep you warm if it was cool. We got to go out on a truck with a guide who would point out places where we would see elephants, lions, cheetahs, and leopards.

I must have watched the great migration on TV a thousand times, but when you see it in person, it's a whole different thing. At the Serengeti in Tanzania, we went out for three days in a row in trucks and the guides said, "No, they're not ready yet," and we'd all come back. The animals were waiting for something—nobody really knows what—before they'd start. You could see the crocodiles waiting in the river, the buzzards waiting above. And then suddenly the first wildebeest jumped out and they all followed. In person you can smell the odor of death from the wildebeests and zebras and other animals that get eaten by the crocs and the big cats as they start their trek across the Serengeti. It was beautiful and terrible.

I could not get it out of my mind. It got me thinking about what it means for us humans—what it meant for me—to follow the herd and do what everyone else was doing. Those zebras and wildebeests were jumping into a river full of crocs waiting to eat them, just because all the other animals around them were doing it. How many of us humans are jumping into those dangerous waters too? This idea struck me so deep that I wrote a poem about it.

You could've been in a herd,
not understanding a single word,
playing follow the leader, just a grass-eating breeder,
watching for predators in the grass,
knowing that they're after your ass,
your only purpose on this earth,
is to be part of the food chain and giving birth.
But no you're human, you have a brain,
you have a choice to come in out of the rain.
You were blessed with a soul, you have a goal,

you can go to school, and learn the Golden Rule.
'Cause if you don't think for yourself,
you can't blame no one else,
so whatever you do with your life,
you're the captain of your happiness or strife.
In your life you have a choice,
to listen, or not listen, to that inner voice.
Back in the game it was called mother wit,
It would sometimes let you miss the bullshit,
that's if you would take heed
and not give into your selfish greed.
But whatever you make up your mind to do,
just remember it's all up to you.
It better be fast, 'cause it goes in a flash.
Get you swimming in the head,
and then you're dead,
and then it's too late to look back,
'cause that's all she wrote, Jack.

The animals end their migration at the Maasai Mara National Reserve in Kenya, so we went there next and hung out with the Maasai warriors in their camps. They totally lived off their cows. Their huts were made of cow dung, and they drank the cows' blood. We watched as they stuck a cow in a vein and then somehow quickly closed up the hole so that the cow would not lose much blood. (No, I did not try some.) The Maasai are very tall—over seven feet—and they have a traditional dance called the *adamu* where they jump straight up in the air to show their strength and impress the girls. Sarah took a lot of photos, and the funny thing was the Maasai were taking pictures of her with their cell phones while Sarah was taking pictures of them.

When we got home, I started on my next album. Our apartment was around the corner from Jimi Hendrix's old studio, Electric Lady, so I could walk to the studio every day while I was recording my doo-wop album, *My True Story*, for Blue Note Records. A lot of really cool doo-wop singers backed me up on the vocals, including Bobby Jay (who used to sing with Frankie Lyman), Joel Katz, Earl Smith Jr., Eugene Pitt, David Johnson, and Dickie Harmon (from the Connotations). Singing with them reminded me of when I started doing doo-wop in the Calliope, sitting on the benches and harmonizing. We had George Receli on drums, Greg Leisz on guitar, and Benmont Tench on keyboards. It was a thrill for me walking to the studio every day and working on that album with all those home run hitters.

My True Story was coproduced by Don Was and Keith Richards from the Rolling Stones. Don produced a lot of the Stones' albums, and he told me when he was working on one of them years ago, he was in the hotel room above Keith's and heard him playing "My True Story" by the Jive Five on a loop, over and over. Since he knew Keith was really into the doo-wop scene, Don asked him if he'd like to coproduce my record. Keith said, "What took you so long, mate?"

Keith and I had stayed friends since we toured with the Stones in the 1980s, and in 2013 when the Rolling Stones sang in Philadelphia, they asked me to sing "Under the Boardwalk" with them. I remember me and Sarah and my manager were sitting up in a sky-box at the theater, just hanging out before the show, and Keith stopped by. He told us, "I think Mick's a little nervous, we've got a singer in the house tonight."

Keith played guitar on all the cuts on *My True Story*. He is one of the most down-to-earth guys I have ever met. He's a great big star, but it doesn't come over like that. I can still listen to that album and smile and think about the sessions and all the guys who played on it. We went in with twenty-one songs and recorded twenty-three in five days. As Keith would say, "Bunch of hard musicians acting like kids." It went so fast and we did so few takes that it was like the 1950s.

When we were in the studio, Keith told me it made him feel like a kid, doing all those old doo-wop songs. We are close to the same age, and we talked about the music we used to listen to when we were kids. It turned out to be a lot of the same stuff, especially from the doo-wop era. We talked about me and Artie's records from the 1960s that Keith liked, and a lot of other great New Orleans singers he listened to, like Ernie K-Doe, Irma Thomas, Bennie Spellman, and Lee Dorsey.

Keith said he bought most of my early records in England. I felt like I'd been punched in the gut when he said that, because Minit told me those records never sold no farther than Baton Rouge. Which meant they had been doing international deals all along and never telling me about it—as in, never paying me for my share of the sales. Their lawyer used to tell me what to do, and I did it. It's a hard thing to learn how many people have been cheating you all along. Like Bob Dylan once wrote, you're just a pawn in the game.

That same year, 2013, I fell in love again. This time it was with a shih tzu–pomeranian puppy. I wasn't really looking for a dog, but Sarah wanted one. When we saw him, I told her, "You'd better get him tonight, because he's so cute that someone else will grab him quick." He was so tiny that I could hold him in the palm of my hand, and he had these great big round, innocent eyes that stole my heart. We named him Apache, after me.

I love our cats, but Apache is more like a little boy in a dog suit. He understands more than some humans. His personality is big as a house, and although he has the kindest little heart ever, he knows just how to manipulate us both. I don't like to admit it, but he controls me; I am his manservant.

Apache doesn't like to be without me, so I take him out and around with me—sometimes in bright orange booties and a stylish sweater. He's been backstage at a bunch of concerts (in the VIP area, of course!), and been out on a lot of gigs with me. He's a road dog. I didn't know I could fall for an animal like that, but he proved me very wrong.

When I moved to New York, I started watching mass on TV and saying my rosary every day. It was part of cleaning up my life some. And I walked uptown every Sunday to go to mass at St. Frances of Assisi Church on Thirty-First Street. I know I've done some bad things, and I also know St. Jude saved me from some even worse things. From my Catholic upbringing through my years of wrestling with addiction, God has always been close to me, even the times I've been running away from Him.

Going back over some of my travels, through some dangerous terrain, I know I would not have made it without Jesus holding my hand. He's kept me going, and I wasn't expecting any recognition for that. So I was really surprised when I was awarded the University of Notre Dame's 2015 Laetare Medal, which goes to a Catholic "whose genius has ennobled the arts and sciences, illustrated the ideals of the Catholic Church and enriched the heritage of humanity."

The president of Notre Dame, Reverend John Jenkins, said, "Aaron Neville proudly embraces and honors his faith through his God-given musical talents. Through tumultuous times in his life, Aaron turned to God, the Blessed Virgin Mary, and St. Jude for strength, forgiveness, and salvation. His example of repentance and devotion shine bright for all who see him perform."

It was an honor and a half to receive this medal, which has also been awarded to John F. Kennedy, Helen Hayes, Sister Helen Prejean, Dave Brubeck, and Martin Sheen. They present it at the Notre Dame graduation, and me and Sarah went together. I gave a short speech and then sang "Ave Maria" a capella.

I said, "I am honored and humbled to be receiving such a prestigious medal. I hope I'm worthy of standing next to the people that received it before me. If it's for me trying to get my life on the right track the way God wanted me to, then I am worthy. Because I know, and God knows, that I've tried. I've asked to see the world through God's eyes, and asked that the world sees God in me. My life before has been a preview of where I am now. It took who I was and where I came from to make me who I am."

Then I thanked my parents and the nuns at St. Monica's Catholic School, and one in particular, Sister Damien, for giving me morals and guidance, and I thanked the powerful women in my life, Joel Roux Neville and Sarah Ann Friedman.

I'm so happy that Sarah came into my life and rescued me. I can remember when we started dating, whenever we talked on the phone or met up, it would make me swoon. Here it is, fifteen years later, and she still makes me swoon. Sometimes I see her walking out to the greenhouse or to the kitchen, and it gives me a tingling sensation. Sarah helped me get my life back together after Joel passed, and she backed up off her own career to help me get my life on track. She's Wonder Woman in disguise, my last earth angel.

"Prescient" is a word someone brought to my attention when I let them hear a recording of a song I did at a live show in the mid-'80s at St. Anne in Brooklyn. They asked me if I was singing it to Sarah, and I said no, I was with Joel then. They said the song was prescient. I'd never heard that word before. But now that I know it, I think it was prescient. The song was "And I Love You So" by Don McLean, and there's a part that says I know how lonely life can be, but that my life began again the day I met you.

That's how Sarah Ann makes me feel every day.

23

Apache

I started writing poetry in the 1960s to get through the adversities in my life, and found that it would help me confront big issues and get them out of my system. I wrote poems about our Uncle Big Chief Jolly when I sat in the hospital holding his hand and praying, and I wrote poems after he passed. I wrote one called "Just Make It Go Away" when I was watching Joel's battle with lung cancer.

When I see or hear something that touches my heart, I have to write about it. It could be something I see on the street, a song, a memory, or even a movie or TV show; if it leaves me with a big feeling, good or bad, I write about it. I still write poems about my life with Joel, poems about life on the streets. I write poems about junkie life, jailhouse shit, things I have gone through, things I have seen other people go through.

I write poems about the tough shit people experience so I can pass them on to my children and the kids in the neighborhood, hopefully helping to guide them in some way. I write about my connection with God and how He makes me feel. I write about my beautiful Sarah Ann. I write when I am down and when I am up. It's a kind of therapy for me.

I just write, and the words always come to me like someone is telling them to me. I never could sit down and plan to write—it doesn't happen like that. I have to be inspired.

I used to keep my poems on little scraps of paper that I stuffed into a paper bag, thinking they weren't worth anything. One day I mentioned it to Lynn Batson at the Uptown Youth Center, and she asked to see some of them. She read my poems and typed them out and put them in a notebook for me. I always thought they were trash, but she thought they were great and worth saving. So then I started keeping a poetry journal. Eventually, my poetry journal migrated to a Blackberry (remember those?), and then to my iPhone, where it still lives, because by the time I try to find a scrap of paper sometimes the thought will be gone.

Poetry has a kind of music in it, and I always wanted to bring that music out. So while I would love for you to read my poetry, I also really dig singing it. Through the years several of my poems have become songs, often with the collaboration of my brothers or other musicians who helped me work out the music that I already heard in the words. These are the songs of my life. If you listen to the lyrics, you'll know my story in a way that's different from reading this book, but just as true.

I've already told you about "Yellow Moon." I wrote "Brother Jake" about me and Cyril's friend Jake (a.k.a. Alfred Rudolph) hoboing across the country after he, Cyril, and myself had a run-in with the police in an alley between two barrooms. I said in the song that he had to ride the rails, which meant he was hopping freight cars around the country. When he came back to New Orleans, he got into a fight near the Magnolia Projects, down around the area where you score. The guy hit him on the head, and it killed him when he fell onto the curb. I wrote that song because Jake was like a brother to me and Cyril.

The song called "Voodoo," me and Marvin and Stackolee and Lil Red were in the First District Police Station (auto theft again—cars were just too easy to steal), and there was this older Black woman who had been brought in, I don't know for what. They were trying to get her in a cell and she refused to go in. She kept saying, "Don't put your hands on me. I'm calling on Magnolia, Father Black Heart, and Mother Dora." They were scared to touch her, so they asked us to help them put her in the cell. We said, "No way! We're not touching that lady." So they let her stay out in the walk-around until she got released. I don't know anything about Voodoo, but because it's a part of New Orleans, I wrote a song about it.

After seeing so many guys out on the streets, I wrote "My Brother's Keeper." And when I needed God in my life, I wrote "Steer Me Right Sweet Jesus." Sometimes I would think about my days of using drugs and would write poems like "Lil' Junkie Boy" and "Mr. Jones." You don't wanna meet up with Mr. Jones while skipping and flipping through those mean streets.

When Joel left in 1972, I wrote a song called "Cradle Days" that Bette Midler recorded. It went:

You took me from my mother's loving arms
I still had about a foot to grow
I don't believe that I had made seventeen
But girl I loved you so.
Actually we raised each other;
You, our kids and myself
You wait till they become a part of me
And you put me on the shelf

Sarah helped me gather up some of my poems into a book called *I Am a Song*, which I published in 2010. And she helped me do something else really important to me that year too: start the Aaron Neville Quintet.

By the time I moved to New York, the Neville Brothers had recorded our last album together. We did keep touring some until 2015, but the Neville Brothers needed to play a lot to make a lot, and we were all tired of being out on the road three or four weeks at a time. And besides, I've never seen an armored truck behind a funeral. Your money can't save you. After Artie had two back surgeries, it was time for him to get off the road. And it was getting harder for me to hit those high notes when I couldn't even take a deep breath when my asthma was flaring up. Plus my back would hurt when I'd come off stage from trying to breathe. I used to make a joke about it. I'd say, "Did y'all see who was behind me kicking me in my back?" It was time to call it a halt. But I had something deep inside that I still wanted to get out. I was ready to do my solo thing full time while I still had voice enough to do it.

Our manager was just looking for the easy money with more Neville Brothers and thought he wouldn't make any money with me as a solo act. It was like the shit from early in my career was happening all over again—the manager wanted to keep control of me and was passing up good opportunities for the same old same old. Our manager was saying that there wasn't any outlet for my solo career, but that turned out to be dead wrong. There were plenty of Aaron Neville fans waiting for it.

Sarah pushed me to make a move to Red Light Management. They made an offer to the Brothers to come along with me, but they declined. Artie was still playing with the Funky Meters, Cyril was doing other things with Brothers of the Wetlands and New Orleans Indian bands, so I started the Aaron Neville Quintet and had the chance to do the music I yearned to do. The quintet played softer, so I didn't have to sing loud, and I could change keys to make it easier to hit the notes; it felt like a luxury.

The Aaron Neville Quintet featured my brother Charlie, the horn man; plus Michael Goods on keyboards and vocals; Earl Smith Jr. on drums and vocals; David Johnson on bass, keyboards, and vocals; and a couple of different really talented guitar players at different times: Eric Struthers, Makuni Fukuda, Jamie McLean, or Shane Theriot (who Artie used to call Shane the Riot). We ended up touring all over the world, including a return trip to New Zealand.

With the quintet I could actually hear my brother Charles playing his horn and everyone taking their solos. I could do the songs I
liked that were too quiet for the Neville Brothers, like "Stardust"
and "Mona Lisa." We still had that fierce funkiness, but it was a
more intimate version of it. It was a special band. We had a lot of
fun, too. Everybody was smiling on the stage and we could clown
around a little bit with the music. It was really groovy.

Then in 2011, Sarah came up with the idea of doing some duo
shows with just me and Mike, my pianist, and that turned out to be
way cool. Mike and I had done a couple of duo shows before, but
we hadn't really made it official. The first time we performed just
the two of us was at the Fillmore West in San Francisco way back
in 1999, when we were opening for John Lee Hooker. John Lee
Hooker had a big band with him, but it was just me and Mike—
the dynamic duo. Mike was scared shitless and was fumbling at the
piano. If he made a mistake, I would just make it funny and get
people laughing. After we got through the gig, he said, "Man, I
wasn't even there." But we got three standing ovations. So why not
keep it going?

We did play some bigger places, but for the duo I loved being in
small clubs. It was so intimate, such close interaction with the audience, that I could whisper the songs out. Me and Mike would
rehearse over the phone. It was awful sound, but it worked; we'd go
to gigs ready.

I like the energy of the quintet, and I also like the laidback qual-
ity of the duo, just coming off the top of my head with things, not
having to worry about whether we rehearsed it. People would call

out songs, and if Mike and I knew them, we'd do them. And I'd bring the audience back to where I first started with some Nat King Cole or anything that came to my mind.

I've got about ten million songs in my head. Some of them wake me up at three in the morning, and I've got to sing the whole song to myself before I can get back to sleep, to make sure I know all the words. So sometimes I'd put Mike on the spot because I'd come up with a song he'd never heard before. But then I'd sing a few phrases and he'd catch it and that made it even cooler.

With my own record label, I was able to record what I wanted. I made albums of classic R&B, devotional songs—whatever I was moved to do. As much as I love singing those songs and as much as I am so grateful that I had a chance to record them, my mind kept coming back to my poetry—the journal of the rhythm of my life.

I told Marc Allan at Red Light Management that I wanted to turn some of my poetry into songs, so he hooked me up with two very groovy guys. One was Eric Krasno (a.k.a. Kraz), a talented producer and a guitarist with some retro-funk bands like Lettuce and Soulive. Eric played with my son Ivan in his band, Dumpstaphunk, too. The other was Dave Gutter, a composer and singer with the band Rustic Overtones. They helped me turn nine of my poems (plus two songs by Kraz and Dave, "Be Your Man" and "I Wanna Love You") into songs that all came together on the album *Apache*.

I'm part Choctaw on both sides of my family. I have a picture of my grandmother right next to a picture of Geronimo, and they look like they could be sister and brother. They have the same nose and high cheekbones, and I have them too. When I was in my late teens, in the summer I'd be outside, and my skin would turn red from the sun. Plus I used to wear my hair straight down with a headband around it. So the guys in the neighborhood started calling me Apache Red, and then I just shortened it to Apache. It's always been my nickname.

My license plate on my big old T-bird in New Orleans was Apache, my dog is named Apache, and around 2015 a tattoo artist in New York City came up to my terrace and tattooed it across my back. Apache is me. It's the perfect name for this album.

When Kraz and me started talking, we knew we wanted to take it back to the soul funk era of the late '60s and early '70s. We talked about "Hercules," which I recorded back in 1973 with the Meters, and how much we liked that sound. But I remember hearing my brother Artie saying that he didn't want to be pigeon-holed as a funkster or an R&B band. I feel the same way. I love (and have recorded) every kind of music you can think of. And I wanted to do all of it—plus give it something fresh and new—on *Apache*.

Most of the instruments and gear we used on *Apache* were made before 1975, so we could get that retro vibe, but Kraz also used a lot of modern studio tricks to get us where we wanted to go. That album could be called *The Other Side of Aaron*, because people who know me from doing the ballads and New Orleans stuff were getting another feel on *Apache*. It was something old and something new. I was hoping people who might not even know my music would get turned on to it.

Kraz got together a lot of guys he'd played with, and they were outstanding, no exceptions. It was a pleasure to play with them, including Adam Smirnoff on guitar, Ryan Zoidis on sax, Eric Bloom on trumpet, Adam Deitch on percussion, Nigel Hall on vocals, and the wind section from the amazing Sharon Jones and the Dap-Kings (including David Guy on trumpet and Cochemea Gastelum on all sorts of wind instruments). Most of these guys weren't even born when "Tell It Like It Is" came out fifty years earlier, but they brought the funk nevertheless.

Tell It Records, my company, was making the album, so I wasn't at the mercy of anyone else's idea about what it should sound like. Nothing ended up on *Apache* that I didn't want to be there. But we were all thinking about the music the same way. It was pure joy getting up every morning and going to the studio in Brooklyn to work with Kraz and the band. And that's me playing the piano on a couple of tracks.

The songs on *Apache* are like a journey through my life and my heart. It's like this book, but told in poetry and music.

"All of the Above," "Orchid in the Storm," and, of course, "Sarah Ann" are all about Sarah, my beautiful earth angel. "All of the Above" is pure confunktion. After we did the vocal tracks, Cochemea Gastelum added some slinky sax. The song asks,

Is it a physical attraction?
Is it sexual satisfaction?
Is it long life together?
Going through all kinds of weather?
Is it holding each other's hands?

Making all kinds of plans?
Never, never saying goodbye
Never, never making each other cry
Love is all the above

"Orchid in the Storm" I would call a rock R&B song. Cochemea hit it again with a really pretty flute solo on this one.

You're the rose among the thorns
You're the diamond in the dirt
You're my orchid in the storm
I can't see living without you
You're the beating in my heart
Been right there from the start
I can't see living without you

"Sarah Ann" is pure doo-wop, like an old Drifters song. It features a sweet organ solo by Peter Levin. The song starts out,

When you first took my photograph
You were a friend you even made me laugh
All through some trying times
You even took away the crying
You are my saving grace
I love looking in your pretty face
You saw straight to my soul
Took me to have and to hold

Oh sweet Sarah Ann
With your lens you saw right thru me
You saw everything that I could be
You save me from my hell
You picked me up when I fell
I wanna wake up with you every day
When I do I want to hear you say
You'll always be mine
Forever till the end of time

"Heaven" is my version of a spiritual. It's kind of a plea I made to God: If I ever caused anybody harm, I'm sorry.

God forgive me
For any wrong I've done
Please forgive me
If I ever hurt anyone
And save a little place in heaven for me

"Hard to Believe" is what I would call a hard rock song. It starts out with a hard bass beat and then the horns bust in. This song gives you a sense of how unsafe I felt, especially after Katrina.

What's waiting 'round the corner
What's lurking 'round the bend
Is it the beginning
The beginning of the end

Should I turn around
Or keep straight ahead
Get up, see what's outside
Or just stay in bed

"Ain't Gonna Judge You" is about all kinds of judgment—Black and white, rich and poor, junkies, people in jail. I never really cared about that stuff, but I see how it goes in the world. In the song I'm saying people should tend to their own business; don't judge me and I won't judge you. The music here gets into some heavy funk, and the horns—mostly from the Dap-Kings—really blast it out.

Can't tell a book by the cover
It ain't no front-page news
Respect one another
You look at me up and down
Take a closer look at yourself
You can judge me all you want

In "Make Your Momma Cry" I was talking about myself and the ways I brought heartache on both Mommee and Poppee. Listening to it makes me think about when my grandmother Maw Maw told someone in her Creole accent that if they kept doing what they were doing, their ass was gonna drag the ground. She said, "I might be dead and gone, but the red ants will bring me the news."

One verse says,

Why in the world you wanna be so bad
Give heart trouble to your dear old dad
Thinking you're the baddest man around
Soon they're going to plant you in the ground
Trouble gonna run you down

Another one says,

You and your friends better stop stealing all of them cars
'Fore you locked up behind them bars
Sure as you're born you were bound to die
So wipe that tear from your momma's eye

You look at the news and it gives you the blues. That's where "Fragile World" came from. Hurricane Katrina was bad, but you look around the world and so many disasters are going on everywhere. It looks like the Earth is saying, "Man, you've been misusing me all these years, and I'm fighting back now. I'm pissed at you." I have a couple of shout-outs to Marvin Gaye on that song; he saw what was happening too and where it was all gonna take us.

"Fragile World" is spoken word while the band plays behind me. It was the only way to get my words across. I wanted the album to be like "Hercules," but with how things are going in the world this song is more like "Herculess." By the way, that's my funky knuckle piano in the background; you don't read no music, you just play what's in your head.

Fragile world
Everyone's in the path
So no one's safe from its mighty wrath
Tornadoes, earthquakes, and hurricanes
Forest fires, mudslides, torrential rain
Heat waves, floods, and blizzards
Melting the polar ice
And if all that's not bad enough
Humans just won't play nice

If *Apache* is my life in an album, "Stompin' Ground" is my life in one song. It runs down everything about where I come from, like I painted you a picture of New Orleans with me in it. I call out all the New Orleans places and people that are important to me. If you've read this far, you'll recognize a lot of them.

There's Calliope, Magnolia, and Melpomene—housing projects that aren't there anymore. It's people that tore them down, not Katrina. We didn't have to worry about no hurricanes back in those days because those old bricks withstood anything.

I gave a shout-out to Billy Beat the World, Scarface John, and Mac Rebennack. Billy Beat the World is a boy I was in the parish prison with. Scarface John was the guy I sang about with the Wild Tchoupitoulas in the song "Brother John Is Gone." Mac Rebennack, that's Dr. John. He and I are the same age, and I used to hang out and do a little dope with him back in the day. Way back then, Mac was a guitar player, but he got shot in the finger and that's when he started making the piano his main instrument.

James Booker I've mentioned already; he was one of the greatest piano players who ever walked the planet. Professor Longhair, Fats Domino, and Satchmo you know too. Big Chief Jolly, that's my Uncle Jolly with the Wild Tchoupitoulas. Ratty Chin? That's my brother Cyril. Art the Mighty Row is my brother Art. Horn Man is my brother Charles.

Not everyone name-checked in "Stompin' Ground" is so famous, but they're famous to me. Like Treacherous Slim and Second-Line Black and Stackolee. Jab, he was just a dope dealer back in the day. Marvin and Johnny Metoyer were two of my close running buddies who you've met already. And Mole Face and Melvin—well, you know all about those two.

Every time I call their names, I can see their faces and remember where I met them and what we were doing. We were all like a tribe. I wish I had pictures of all those characters.

The song itself is pure New Orleans funk. Adam Deitch played phenomenal drums, giving it a spare, cool Indian beat. He told us his poppa and momma both played drums, and drums are like a second skin to him. I didn't have to tell him nothing; he just felt it.

When *Apache* came out in 2016, a lot of people said it was my best album ever. *Apache* was like my whole recording career wrapped up in a bow.

That year I celebrated my seventy-fifth birthday with a smoking-hot concert at Brooklyn Bowl. Dumpstaphunk, Ivan's band, kicked it off, along with George Porter Junior and Runnin' Pardners. Dr. John set the stage on fire, and Kraz came out and played with me. I invited Paul Simon, who I'd played with before, to perform, and after his rehearsal we got to talking. We were both born the same year, and we started reminiscing about shooting marbles as kids and listening to doo-wop and how that music just ran through us so sweet. And suddenly we were back in this world where we seemed to have the same childhood. Paul is a white, Jewish guy who grew up in Queens, New York, and I'm a Black dude who grew up in a New Orleans housing project, but the songs and sounds that were in our heads were so similar.

Awhile after the album came out, I flew down to New Orleans and recorded "Stompin' Ground" again with the Dirty Dozen Brass Band for the movie *Take Me to the River: New Orleans* (which, if you want to know about the New Orleans music scene, that movie is all you need). My son Ivan, my brothers Charles and Cyril, and my nephew Ian (Artie's son) were at that session with us. George Porter, the bass player from the Meters, was there too.

When the movie soundtrack came out in 2022, the song got nominated for a Grammy in the category Best American Roots Performance. "Stompin' Ground" is all about my roots in New Orleans, so you can't get more American roots than that. I knew it was that type of song—so truthful, so from the heart, so real—that we had the potential to win.

I didn't go to the Grammys, so on a cold night in February 2023 me and Sarah watched on a livestream as they gave out the awards.

As we snuggled up I was thinking about how Sarah preserved me to be able to still be here, to let me do so much more in my life, to be nominated for another Grammy. About how she put her career on hold while she saved mine.

When we won, my heart jumped. It made me feel like a kid again. I'm eighty-two years old and retired, and I just won my fifth Grammy. Possibly not my last, either.

24

Freville Farm

In 2015, soon after I finished recording *Apache*, Sarah and I had a chance to sell our New York City apartment for a good deal, so we bought a twelve-acre farm in New York's Hudson Valley. Sarah had already been growing food and flowers in pots on our terrace in the city, which I started calling Freville Farm as a kind of joke. Now she put together the whole farm, from tilling the soil to planting every kind of food you could think of—asparagus to tomatoes, cucumbers, okra, watermelon, corn, strawberries, raspberries, potatoes, turmeric, ginger, garlic. She hooked up the irrigation system. She raises chickens and figured out how to keep them safe from the local wildlife without hurting the animals. And she's brought thousands of eggs and food plants to the local resource center. I'm amazed every time I look at the farm she's built for us.

Me and Mike kept the duo touring. I was supposed to go to California in February of 2020, but Sarah saw all the shit that was happening there with COVID and said it was gonna be bad. People were telling her, "Oh no, it's not gonna be bad," but as usual, she was right. She thought it was not a good idea for me to be flying six hours on a plane with people who could be infected. Then I started thinking about how they were testing people and putting them in quarantine if they had a fever, and I started to picture myself somewhere far away from home being put into quarantine and possibly never seeing Sarah or my family again.

When COVID shut everything down, I finally retired. The epidemic helped me realize that time is precious, and that with my asthma, it was time for me to step back and sit down. I'm eighty-two years old and I don't have the wind I had before. I don't want to be onstage singing and not sounding like Aaron Neville. I've got no regrets about that. I have enough recordings out there.

I've sung on most of the famous stages in the world, including Carnegie Hall, the Kennedy Center, and the Sydney Opera House. I've performed at all the jazz festivals, including the North Sea Jazz Festival, Berlin, and of course, New Orleans. I've sung at the White House. I've appeared on all the TV talk shows, and on *Sesame Street*. I have songs in movies, and I've even been in a couple of movies myself.

I've also traveled the world, and now it's time to stay in one place. Being home the last three years has really made me see how blessed I am not having to travel, just hanging with my shmoops— Sarah Ann, my little bitty buddy Apache, Turks and Caicos, and

Grace Slick, a cat who wandered onto the farm one day and decided to live with us. I do think about the shows I did with my brothers, and my quintet, and the duo with Mike, and all of the fans who showed me so much love on our gigs; the meet and greets, the autograph signings, hanging in the green rooms that were never green. It's a nice memory. But I don't miss the Airport Agony or being stuck in buses and hotels. Sarah told me about this phrase her father would say, "Let's not and say we did." I use it a lot these days. (Thanks, Dr. Friedman.)

Being out here on the farm every day gives me a lot of time to just look at nature and think. I think a lot about God and how amazing He is. All the things I watch Sarah raising in the garden and greenhouse, helping to water the plants and watch them grow— life comes from a little seed and a lot of tender love and care. I see how the trees just hang out together, never arguing or hating on each other, the different looks to the sky, the formation of the clouds, the hard and soft rain. All the little creatures I see on the ground and in the grass, they all have a purpose in God's world. The grass grows back healthy even after the harshest of weather, months of snow, months of high heat.

It's so peaceful just staring out the window—it's always different. I like seeing the little birds running the big bully bird away from their nests, hearing the birds singing in the mornings and afternoons, the beautiful sunrises and sunsets, the four seasons. I sit out in the yard with Sarah and Apache and feel God's presence, take each day as it comes, take whatever it brings. I just wish the whole world could be as peaceful.

I'm sure thankful to God for letting me use His voice all those years, and enabling me to bring so much joy to folks everywhere in the world, and for letting it be with me in dire times to comfort my own self. It felt so good to stand onstage anywhere and see how our music soothed so many souls, including ours. When my two older brothers left us, Artie and Charles, that was a heavy blow. I know they are in heaven now, gigging with all the other greats in that heavenly band.

I never thought I would be here for this long. All the times I almost took myself out with the drugs, God brought me back, saying, "Oh no, young fellow, I'm not gonna let you get out like that." I give many thanks for it all—all that God blessed me to be able to do, the longevity He let me have while watching so many of my friends fall by the wayside. Sometimes I wonder why. But who am I to question God?

I know I made a lot of great music in my life, and it's forever on records for the world to listen to. Whenever I was singing, each note was coming from a place that I had lived myself or witnessed in someone else, the joy and the pain. Like the saying goes, "They that sings, prays twice." My soul is satisfied.

People sometimes ask me to describe my voice. I say that it's the strength of my father, the tenderness of my mother, and the innocence of my childhood, and all the things I've done in my life that have let me have compassion for the people I met on my journey. Each note tells the story of a happy time, a sad time, a lonely time, a hurtful time of my life, and other people's hurt and pain that I saw or felt. I listen and can feel it all in my voice, like reliving it. Like my song says, it took who I was and where I came from to make me who I am.

I give God all praise and thanks for steering me through. Sometimes I would pray and didn't think I was being answered, but I know now sometimes no answer is actually an answer. So when I see or hear of someone going down that same highway, I send them a prayer that somehow they can come out on the other side.

From the goodness I received from my family to some of the demons I tried to fight off in my boyhood and my young man days, I know how easy it is to get trapped in the game. I was trapped for quite some time. I know the good, the bad, and the ugly about it all because I lived it. I do believe that God was with me all the way, through some hellfired treacherous mean streets. I did and saw a whole lot—so much ain't no tongue could tell. Believe me, it was a crazy journey, but I do not regret it because I know I was supposed to do and see a lot of those things so that I could have compassion and empathy for others who were going through a lot of the same adversities.

My father used to tell me, "Don't wind up a lost ball in the high weeds, 'cause after a while people stop looking for that lost ball and get a new one." At times I was lost like that, but I never gave up on God and He never gave up on me. Instead, He gave me a tool—a song to sing and a voice to sing it with—and I thank Him from the bottom of my heart. I guess there was a reason that He brought me this mighty long ways.

I used to say I wished I could hit a note so pure that it cured cancer. And who knows? Maybe I have. There was a little autistic boy in Las Vegas—his family told me about him. He flapped around like a seal, and they said the only thing that would calm him was a headset with my voice playing. That's the God in me touching the God in him. I don't take credit for that. People tell me what my voice has done for them, and I say, "I wish I could tell you what it has done for me."

I sometimes sit and reminisce about my eighty years here on planet Earth, and my time playing music with my brothers and my quintet and duo, my ups and downs, ins and outs, and as I look back on it all, no regrets. Well, maybe just a few.

Sometimes I have a tear in my eye thinking about how I must have hurt my parents with some of the choices I made in my young life. My father died at fifty years old, and I just pray it wasn't from a broken heart. I think about hurting Joel with my choice to do drugs, when she went to live with her parents and had to hear from her father, "I told you so." I look back and ask God's forgiveness, and my family's forgiveness, but there's nothing I can do about it now but pray. There's no point in thinking about what I would do if I had the chance to go back, because that's impossible.

Now that I'm past eighty, I have come to realize that there's no such thing as old people. We become older children. Because I know I never grew up—that little kid is forever in my heart. I may not run as fast or jump as high as I used to, or do some of the stupid stuff I used to do, but I'm still walking fast and jumping just a little. I still have memories of my childhood, and that child still lives in my heart. I can hear a certain song, and a face and a time immediately springs into my mind. I can think of a book my mother read a story to me from. I'm so thankful that I met all the folks along my journey, and am still meeting people. So the child in me says thank you, Lord, for my longevity, thank you for the kid still in my heart.

I don't long for days gone by. I love the days I'm in right now.

Acknowledgments

I want to first thank the Lord Jesus and St. Jude Thaddeus, the saint of impossible and hopeless cases, my parents, my brothers and sister, my children, and Marc Allan and Daniel Romanoff of Red Light Management. I want to thank Beth Adelman for helping me write this book of my life. I want to thank Lauren Marino, Mary Ann Naples, Michelle Aielli, Michael Barrs, and the entire team at Hachette Book Group, and Jeff Kleinman and Steve Troha at Folio Literary Management. I want to thank all of my musician friends from the Neville Brothers band and from the Aaron Neville Quintet, and John Brenes of the Music Coop Record Store in Ashland, Oregon. And last but not least, my wife and best friend, Sarah Ann Friedman. Without her being in my life, none of this would be possible. She helped me in so many ways. I thank God for sending her into my life and helping me cross quite a few hurdles. To all my fans who supported me through my career, I hope you all enjoy reading about my journey through this life.